PU

THE NEW

WIL

For many years, the people of Switzerland suffered under the oppressive rule of a tyrannical emperor. While the royal family enjoyed the fruits of the land, the people starved, breaking their backs to raise enough to pay their taxes. In one province, however, things were changing. The stirrings of rebellion had been heard, and one man in particular was to become the figurehead of the new uprising – William Tell.

At first, Tell was a reluctant hero. Once a mercenary soldier, he had worked as a village blacksmith for many years and his skills as a marksman had lain dormant. But now, spurred into rebellion by the actions of a cruel and ruthless governor, Gessler, Tell's marksmanship with a crossbow was once again to become renowned throughout the land.

This exciting novel by Anthony Horowitz, based on his own scripts for the television series, brings the legend of William Tell to life in a thrilling way.

Anthony Horowitz lives in London. He has written several children's books, including the third Robin of Sherwood book, *The Hooded Man*, with Richard Carpenter.

Also by Anthony Horowitz

Enter Frederick K. Bower
The Falconer's Malteser
Public Enemy Number 2
The Devil's Door-bell
The Night of the Scorpion
The Silver Citadel
Robin of Sherwood: The Hooded Man
(with Richard Carpenter)

THE NEW
ADVENTURES OF

William Tell

Anthony Horowitz

PUFFIN BOOKS

PUFFIN BOOKS

Published by the Penguin Group
27 Wrights Lane, London W8 5TZ, England
Viking Penguin Inc., 40 West 23rd Street, New York, New York 10010, USA
Penguin Books Australia Ltd, Ringwood, Victoria, Australia
Penguin Books Canada Ltd, 2801 John Street, Markham, Ontario, Canada L3R 1B4
Penguin Books (NZ) Ltd, 182–190 Wairau Road, Auckland 10, New Zealand

Penguin Books Ltd, Registered Offices: Harmondsworth, Middlesex, England

First published 1989

Printed and bound in Great Britain by
Cox & Wyman Ltd, Reading
Filmset in Linotron Palatino by
Rowland Phototypesetting Ltd,
Bury St Edmunds, Suffolk

Contents

One: The Banquet

It all began with a visiting prince, a banquet and a hat on a pole.

The prince was called Frederick, the eldest son of the Emperor – a sallow, pompous man who enjoyed his sense of power without knowing fully how to use it. For him, power meant little more than fine clothes and good food. He liked to surround himself with fawning admirers and never cared that as soon as his back was turned they would speak of him only with contempt. Once a year he would travel across the great kingdom that his father ruled, stopping in each province to visit the castle of the local Governor where he would expect to be entertained . . . royally.

And every Governor would try to outdo the other, providing ever more extravagant entertainments. Frederick was a bore. He drank too much and couldn't hold his drink. He was unpredictable – one minute laughing and showering jewels on the company, the next whining like a six-year-old over some imagined slight. But his father was the Emperor. And one word from the Emperor could strip a man of his wealth and position and send him out into the fields with nothing more than the clothes on his back.

So, as the royal entourage made its way across the land, tables were spread with white silk cloths, loaded with gold and silver plates, rare fruits, expensive spices carried from the east. Haunches of venison turned on spits over blazing fires while minstrels played, jugglers performed and servants and pages ran back and forth from the kitchens, fearful of letting the food cool in the evening air.

And while the fires roared and the music echoed and the banquets went on long into the night, nobody would dare mention, nobody would even think, that outside the castle walls the people were starving and that every minute of every day they cursed the tyranny that gave the royal family all the fruits of the land but kept them in chains.

In one province, however, things were different. The province looked the same as any other. Its villages were small and wretched. The people spent their days out in the fields, up to their knees in mud, breaking their backs to raise enough crops to pay their taxes. At every crossroads, a corpse swung in the wind, hanged for theft, for treason, for any reason that might serve as a warning to the others. But in this province, something was astir. It was not yet a shout. The people were still too afraid. But even so, it was there, a whisper in the wind, or a soft muttering by candlelight as the night clouds drew their cloak over the sun. Rebellion. Revolution. Freedom.

The Governor of that province had heard it and he was afraid. Gessler had been in power now for five years and he had learnt to enjoy his power in a way that Frederick could never have imagined. Whatever he wanted he took, and the more pain he could cause by taking it, the happier he was. It wasn't enough just to steal a farm and use its proceeds to feed himself. He would also turn the farmer out of his house, set him to work as a serf in the fields, perhaps imprison his wife or his daughter for good measure. When Gessler rode through the villages, the streets emptied. Eyes were turned away and faces became pale. And this gave him a surge of irresistible pleasure. That was how things should be. He was more than a Governor. He was a god. Life and death hung on his mood and one command from him could bring absolute destruction.

But now he was worried. It didn't matter to him that the peasants were meeting in secret, questioning his authority. They were no more than animals, following the sun into the fields and returning to their miserable hovels with the darkness. At any other time he would have welcomed their pathetic attempts at insurrection. It would be a perfect excuse to send out his black knights. But for the first time, the Emperor had caught wind of their mutterings too – and that was potentially disastrous. If the Emperor lost faith in him, he could lose everything. That was the trouble with the royal family. It didn't take much to make them nervous.

So the visit of Prince Frederick had a greater significance for Gessler than for the other Governors. By impressing the son, he might impress the father and quell any fears about the running of his province. Gessler was not a stupid man. He knew that he could always have a few peasants whipped or perhaps burn down a village. But that would only demonstrate his power. He needed to prove that his authority was unquestioned.

For several days he mused over the problem. He needed a symbol, something to show that he exercised rigid and total control in his province and that his people were unswerving in their loyalty to the Emperor. He thought about his guest, his love of food and fine clothes. And then an idea came to him. It was a ridiculous idea . . . but perhaps that was its strength. By utterly humiliating his own people, Gessler would prove once and for all that he governed with a fist of iron.

He ordered a hat to be placed on a pole in every village. The hat he chose was an exact duplicate of one that Prince Frederick wore. Anyone who passed the pole would bow to the hat. That was Gessler's command. It would vindicate him and it would flatter Frederick. And the very thought of it, the peasants ludicrously bowing and scraping to a measure of velvet and feather, gave him a curious feeling of pleasure. It was the perfect solution to his problem.

Meanwhile, as Gessler summoned the black knights of his personal guard, a meeting was being held in a run-down tavern in the corner of one of the villages. There were a dozen men in the half-light, crouched over a rough wooden table . . . and one boy. The atmosphere in the room was tense. But nobody was more tense than the boy, who was listening to every word with an anger that shone in his eyes and fought to break free of his clenched fists.

His name was Matthew Tell. His father was the village blacksmith. And it sometimes seemed to Matthew that William Tell was the only man in the country who refused to involve himself in the stirrings of revolt.

'Gessler stole my land. He allowed me to keep one small shed . . . for me and my family. How much longer are we going to let this go on? How much longer are we going to be treated like slaves?'

The speaker was a young man in his early twenties. He had introduced himself as Roland and he travelled with a girl of the same age whom he called Blade . . . perhaps because of the many knives she carried. She was not speaking, but from time to time Roland would glance at her and she would nod, encouraging him to continue.

'We must fight, now. While we still have the strength . . .'

A pitcher of mead had been set down on the table and, his mouth dry with excitement, Matthew reached out to pour himself some. But the earthenware cup was only halfway to his lips when he felt his wrist clasped in a powerful hand. Slowly, the cup was forced back to the table. He turned round to look into the iron-grey eyes of his father.

William Tell had known where to find his son. All he had to do was look for trouble . . . Matthew was sure to be there. And this was trouble all right. He could see it in the faces of the people who were now staring at him, wondering why he was there, questioning why he had not come before.

'I'm sorry to interrupt,' he muttered with a smile. Then, to Matthew, 'The midday meal is on the table.'

Matthew hated being treated like a child. He was fifteen, old enough to marry, old enough to have children of his own. But he didn't dare argue with his father. It had been said that William Tell was the most violent peaceful man in the kingdom. People spoke of his past, his life as a mercenary fighting against the Emperor but, in truth, little was known. It was said that he had been a great fighter, that his skill with the cross-bow was unparalleled, that he had once led an entire army of his own. But the borders between history and legend are thin and where William Tell was concerned they had become invisible. All that was known for sure was that he was a first-class blacksmith, that he had lived in the village for more than five years and that in all that time he had never once raised a weapon in anger.

He was angry now, however.

'I found him in the tavern – about to down a cup of mead,' he explained as he dragged Matthew into the house. The house was hardly bigger than a single room. In this confined space the family ate, slept, washed and lived together, often sharing it with stray pigs or chickens that happened to wander in.

'Matthew . . . !' His mother was still a beautiful woman, but she was beginning to grow old before her time. Already there were wisps of grey in her hair and her eyes always seemed tired. Hers had been a hard life, made harder perhaps by her knowledge of the man she had married.

'I wanted to hear Roland speak,' Matthew complained. He took his place at the table. 'Gessler stole his land, forced him out of his house.'

'Gessler . . . ! That man is a sin against nature!' This last voice belonged to the village priest, Brother Gregory. He ate wherever anyone would feed him, for he had no family of his own. Despite his tedious sermons and his habit of talking too much even when he was out of the pulpit, he was well-liked. He had been in the village for sixty years, ever since he was a child. 'Somebody ought to run him through and do us all a favour,' he concluded.

'I remember you once told me that those who lived by the sword die by the sword.' Tell cut himself a piece of bread while his wife served a turnip-and-potato stew from a steaming iron pot. 'I gave up fighting so I could get some peace from nagging priests,' he added.

Matthew laughed, but Brother Gregory puffed out his cheeks and lifted his eyebrows indignantly. Tell sighed. The priest always did that before a sermon. It was said that the further his eyebrows rose, the longer the sermon would continue.

'When a mercenary kills for money, that's a sin,' Brother Gregory began. 'But when a man sits idly by as evil princes and potentates invade the land God gave him, strip him of his freedom, plunder the fruits of his labours, tax him to the utter limit of endurance, destroy his family, tear down his house, maltreat his goat and squeeze him like a lemon grown expressly for his own use, that's an even greater sin, William Tell.'

He had not drawn a single breath during this entire sentence and by the end of it his eyes were bulging and his face had gone a curious shade of crimson. But sucking in a great mouthful of air, he went on.

'How long will you turn your eyes away from your responsibilities?' he demanded, smashing his fist on the table and sending a spoon flying.

'There are men in every village, armed and ready to cast off our oppressors. They need an experienced leader, William. I've been a priest all my life. I know nothing of war.'

'And that's why you're so eager to rush headlong into it,' Tell said, his face suddenly serious.

Gregory shook his head. 'I'm in no rush, but the people may be. They won't accept this suppression much longer . . . you mark my words! God will send a spark to the flames of rebellion and men will fight for their freedom.'

'Flames burn down houses and kill innocent people.' Tell shook his head. 'Give me a choice between war and Gessler and I'll take Gessler.'

The food had been served by now and the two men fell silent as Katrina – Tell's wife – took her place at the table. She was a good cook and, with a careful blend of spices, she could make a welcome meal out of even the humblest vegetables. But one person in the room hardly ate anything. Matthew Tell was still thinking of the conversation in the tavern. Roland's defiance and the anger of the other villagers seemed a world away from the calm acceptance of his own father. Had Tell looked into his eyes then, he would have seen tears of disappointment. But behind the tears there was something else. William Tell wouldn't fight. Matthew had learnt to accept that.

But one day he, Matthew Tell, would.

*

The fight began, however, not with Matthew Tell or with William Tell but with Brother Gregory. And it began that same afternoon.

Tell was working in the forge, crafting a shoe for the horse of a wealthy merchant who had been passing through, on his way to a trade fair in a nearby town. As usual, Matthew was helping him, manning the bellows and feeding the fire. The meeting in the tavern had long since broken up and the villagers were hard at work, some of them in the fields, some of them in the little stalls that surrounded the village square. Brother Gregory was in the square too, consoling a widow whose husband had been imprisoned by Gessler for theft. The husband might still be alive. But the fact that he was in one of Gessler's cells meant that the end result would still be the same.

That was when Tyrrol rode into the village.

He was the commander of the black knights, the special force that acted as Gessler's private police. The body of a bear, the face of a gargoyle and the voice of a devil, there was little about Tyrrol that was remotely human. Thirty black knights rode with him. A single maypole stood at the very centre of the square, a reminder of the annual spring celebrations. Tyrrol stopped beside it. Lifting something from his saddle bag, he placed it on the pole. It was a hat.

'Listen to me!' he shouted to the villagers, who were already gathering round him. 'By order of

Gessler, Governor of this province by appointment of his most holy majesty, the Emperor, ruler of this most sacred Empire . . .'

'He's got enough titles to drown a mule,' Brother Gregory muttered.

' . . . this hat, a symbol of the Empire, has been placed at the highest point of this village. Whoever passes it must bow to it and show it every appropriate sign and gesture of respect. This is the law. The penalty for disobedience is death.'

Tyrrol paused, as if waiting for someone to argue. Nobody spoke. He smiled, a hideous smile that displayed a row of uneven, glistening teeth. A wolf's smile.

'All honour and glory to his highness, the Emperor,' he snarled. 'And to this symbol of his most holy rule.'

Brother Gregory stepped forward.

'Pay homage to a hat?' he demanded. 'Sacrilege!'

For a moment nobody spoke. The villagers could hardly believe that this old man could have the courage to defy Gessler's commander. It seemed that Tyrrol couldn't believe it either. His mouth opened but he said nothing. Then, spurring his horse forward, he rode up to the priest.

'Kneel, priest!' he demanded.

'Never!'

Nobody saw where the whip came from. Like some vicious sorcerer, Tyrrol had produced it out of thin air. Now he lashed down with it, the coil of leather slicing into the old man's shoulders. Gregory reeled back, a scream caught at the last moment in his throat. But still he stood on his feet.

'Kneel!' Tyrrol howled.

The whip lashed out for a second time and this time Gregory was forced to the ground. But even as he fell he called out to the villagers. 'Defy these evil men. Kneel only to God!'

Tyrrol struck him again and at last Gregory was silenced, stretched out on the ground, a line of dark red welling through the sackcloth that covered his back. 'Kneel!' Tyrrol cried. 'All of you! Pay homage to the hat!'

The whole village was silent. The villagers gazed at their priest, unconscious on the ground. Then, one after the other, they knelt. Roland was the last to join them. His face was white, bloodless but for the single drop on his lip where he had bitten it through, sharing the old man's pain. This was not the time to start a fight, not with thirty armed knights in the village. But his time would come.

'And now tell me, how did the good people like my taste in hats?'

Gessler was sitting on a terrace of his castle, overlooking a lake. It was a beautiful day, the sun dazzling against the still surface of the water. In one hand he held a silver goblet of wine. Tyrrol, his helmet in his hand, stood next to him, still dusty from his long journey.

'Well enough,' he replied. 'But we needed to spill a little blood first.'

'Oh?'

'An old monk cried blasphemy and tried to incite the others.'

Gessler considered the news. 'Well, show me his head then,' he snapped.

'His head . . . ?'

'Well, I assume you cut it off. Or did you hang him?'

'I . . .' Tyrrol licked his lips. 'I didn't think you'd want to execute a priest.'

'Don't ever think,' Gessler was angry now. He gazed at Tyrrol with watery green eyes, his high cheekbones and long, pointed nose giving him a strange resemblance to a predatory bird. 'The next time anyone even hesitates to obey my law, bring him to me. Whenever, wherever I am. And preferably in a public place. I will make an example of him for the others . . . create an image that will linger in their simple minds for ever. I will give them nightmares they will never wake up from, nightmares that will make them too frightened to sleep. Do you understand what I'm saying?'

Tyrrol had actually understood very little of this, but he nodded anyway. Gessler didn't take kindly to fools. But then he didn't take kindly to anyone. 'Of course, sir,' he said.

'Good.' Gessler raised his goblet and sipped the wine with his eyes closed, relishing the taste and the fact that he had killed the wine-maker only that morning. 'Fear and suppression, Tyrrol,' he murmured. 'The two pillars of good government.'

Far away, on the other side of the castle, a trumpet sounded. Gessler heard the sound and put the wine down. He smiled to himself. Everything was going as he had planned. And Frederick, the Emperor's eldest son, had just arrived.

In the village, where little if anything happened throughout the year, the story of Brother Gregory's defiance had spread like the smallpox. The priest was being cared for by the wise woman whose herbal remedies were as close to medicine as the peasants would ever get, but it was said that his back was cut to ribbons and that his chances of surviving were small. Six soldiers had stayed behind in the village to make sure that nobody else would disobey the new edict and, but for the knowledge that if they were harmed a whole army would follow to take revenge, the villagers would have gladly torn them apart.

And nobody disobeyed. They were too frightened. Whether they were carrying the wheat in from the fields or the water from the well, whether walking or running, they would stop and, while the black knights laughed at their humiliation, bow to the scrap of velvet and feather. A pool of blood, drying in the dust, was a grim reminder of what would happen to them if they refused.

William Tell had heard what had happened but although he was clearly sickened by the fate of his friend, he had not stopped work and had refused even to discuss the matter. The hat on the pole didn't seem to worry him.

'It's a child's game,' he said. 'Nothing more.'

Matthew had worked with him through the afternoon in a cold silence punctuated only by the clang of iron against iron. But at last, as the time came to tidy up for the evening, he could bear it no longer.

'Father,' he whispered, 'I'm ashamed of you.'

William Tell didn't hear him – or if he did, he ignored the comment. But Katrina, who had come into the forge with fresh wood for the fire, straightened up, her eyes wide. 'Matthew!'

Matthew strode forward to his father. 'How can you let them walk over us like this?' he demanded.

Tell looked at his son tiredly, his face streaked with dirt. 'You don't understand,' he said.

'Yes I do. You're afraid of what they can do to you. But I'm not!' Matthew had been holding a broom, sweeping the floor, but now he threw it down and ran out of the forge. Katrina reached out to stop him but he was too fast for her.

Brushing past, he was out and gone before Tell could do anything. For a moment the two of them, husband and wife, stared at each other. Then Tell ran after him.

But he was too late. Matthew had already reached the square. Villagers were still passing by, bowing, on their way home.

'What are you doing, all of you?' Matthew shouted.

The black knights looked up, suddenly interested. They had been growing tired of the game. Nothing had happened for hours and they had begun to wonder how long they were going to have to stay in this wretched village, standing beside their horses. But everything about the boy spelled trouble. And trouble was just what they wanted.

There was a cart parked close to the pole. At the same moment as his father appeared in the square behind him, Matthew leapt onto it and reached up for the hat.

'I'll never bow to a hat!' Matthew yelled. 'Never!'

'Matthew . . .'

Matthew didn't even hear the desperate shout. Already he had plucked the hat off the pole. Now he threw it to the ground, leaping down after it. 'That's where it belongs!' he laughed. He stamped on it with one foot, grinding it into the dust. 'That's where . . .'

He got no further. One of the knights had

already moved forward and, before Matthew could utter another word, a lance rammed into his chest, winding him and throwing him off his feet.

The other knights had spread out to surround him, eager spectators at the ordeal that would surely follow. Tell took in the situation instantly. If he didn't act, and now, his son would be killed in front of his eyes. A knight passed in front of him. Lunging forward, Tell tore the crossbow out of his hands, then elbowed him in the face. The knight tumbled backwards into a trough. But already the first knight had lifted his lance again, this time to smash the boy's skull. In a single movement, Tell aimed and fired. The bolt whistled over Matthew, too fast to see, and found its target in the maypole. Even in this moment of crisis, Tell had chosen not to shed blood. He had aimed at the knight's sleeve. And now the knight was securely pinned to the maypole.

Tell ran forward, his only thoughts for his son. Matthew was lying on the ground, breathless, blood on his chin. Tell swept him up in his arms, cradling him like an infant. Inwardly he was cursing himself. He should have seen this coming. He should have prevented it.

He looked up.

The other four knights had closed in on him. Four loaded crossbows were aimed at him, only inches away. The first knight was struggling to free himself, his face white with fear and anger.

Gently, Tell lowered his son back to the ground. There was nothing more he could do.

It was a good banquet, even by Gessler's standards.

The food was rich and plentiful – as were the guests who sat behind a single long table that stretched across the castle's main courtyard. They were eating under the stars, a feast of wild boar and pheasant, stuffed wood pigeon and venison, a hundred different dishes all served on great golden platters. Minstrels played on the battlements and Ranaldo de Grey, the most celebrated juggler in the land, entertained with the impossible, keeping three balls, two eggs, a hat and a fiery torch all spinning in the air at the same time.

Prince Frederick was seated at the head of the table with Gessler on his immediate right. He had already drunk more than was good for him and would have slipped out of his chair altogether had it not been for the weight of the serving girl who was perched on his knee.

'And who is this fine morsel?' he muttered lasciviously.

The girl giggled and Gessler ignored him. He was in a bad mood. The banquet had cost him more than he liked to think . . . money wasted on such foolish company.

He was not alone in his discomfort. Seated at the far end of the table, an elderly man in a thick velvet gown sat staring at his food without eating any of it. This was the Governor of Ursen, a province that happened to neighbour on Gessler's. Protocol had demanded that he should be there tonight, but he would have preferred to stay at home. He had heard too much about Gessler, stories that made him sick. Next to him, his wife glanced nervously at her husband. She knew what he was thinking. But one word spoken out of place could bring about his downfall. The Emperor was easily offended. She hoped that he would keep his mouth shut, at least until they had left the castle.

'More venison, my lord?'

Gessler slid a plate down the table towards the young boy who was sitting on his right. Gessler did not like children. And he particularly did not like having to address a child as 'my lord'. But this child was different. He was indeed a lord, Prince Martin, Frederick's son and the grandson of the Emperor. He was fourteen years old, with long, fair hair and a pale face. Like the Governor of Ursen, he had eaten little and now refused the venison with a shake of his head. Gessler smiled. So long as this loathsome boy painted a good picture when he got back to his grandpa, Gessler was prepared to do anything.

The minstrels struck up another tune. The juggler added two plates to his bizarre collection. The servants came out with bowls of fruit and more jugs of wine. One of the guests, more drunk than anyone else, fell face forward onto the table and lay still. Somebody laughed. Prince Frederick squeezed the thigh of the servant girl and plucked an apple out of the bowl.

Then William Tell was brought in.

His hands had been tied and there was an ugly bruise on one side of his face. Matthew stood next to him, also tied up, his shirt torn and his hair dishevelled. Four of the black knights from the village guarded them while Tyrrol slipped behind the table and whispered in Gessler's ear.

'And what do we have here?' Prince Frederick demanded, noticing the two prisoners for the first time.

'Two rebels, your majesty.' Gessler waved Tyrrol away. 'The boy had the temerity to knock my hat' . . . he coughed and corrected himself . . . 'your hat into the dust and when my guards punished him, his father attacked them.'

Tell and Matthew stood still, looking at the banqueters without emotion. The serving girl on Prince Frederick's knee reached out and took the apple. 'It seems he stole a crossbow from a soldier, hit him on the head and then shot a bolt at the guard,' Gessler went on. 'Pinned him to a maypole by the sleeve!'

'Marvellous!' Prince Frederick raised an eyebrow. 'We ought to have a demonstration of such skilful shooting.'

'Yes.' Gessler eyed the prisoners thoughtfully.

To his left, the girl took a bite out of the apple. 'Untie him.'

The black knights sprang forward and cut through the ropes that bound Tell and Matthew. The two of them rubbed their wrists, but made no effort to move. Meanwhile, Gessler had leant across Prince Frederick. 'May I?' he demanded.

He held out the hand for the apple, now missing a mouthful, and the serving girl gave it to him. Then, turning the apple in his hand, he moved forward to stand next to William Tell. There was a strange similarity between the two men. They were the same height, with the same colour hair and eyes. They could almost have been mirror reflections, but if so it was a distorting mirror that had taken Tell's good looks and twisted them into a wicked, leering image of himself.

'The death penalty hangs over you,' Gessler hissed. 'But in honour of his majesty, I am willing to spare your life.' He turned to the guards. 'Put the boy over there.'

Struggling, Matthew was led to a pole that stood close to the centre of the courtyard. Once again his hands were tied, but this time behind the pole. Once he was sure that the boy was secure, Gessler walked languidly forward, still turning the apple in his palm.

'Shoot the apple off your son's head and you both go free,' he said.

He stopped beside Matthew and balanced the

apple. At once Matthew shook his head. Gessler caught the apple as it fell and leant forward. 'Do that again and I'll put the apple in your mouth,' he snarled.

Matthew stood rigid. There was nothing he could do. He could feel his heart pounding beneath the rags of his shirt and his mouth was as dry as dust. But clenching his teeth, he forced himself to relax. There is no danger, he whispered to himself. There is no danger. Not when the man with the crossbow is William Tell.

But Tell had other ideas. 'I won't do it,' he said.

Gessler laughed. 'If you won't, I'll find someone who will. Tyrrol perhaps. Or him.' He pointed at the drunken nobleman, still lying face down across the table. 'You do what I say, peasant, or you both die.'

Tell looked around him. There were still two guards behind him and out of the corner of his eye he could see the brute they called Tyrrol, his own crossbow trained on him. Matthew was about twenty yards away, standing quite still, his chest heaving. He ran his eye along the banqueting table. Prince Frederick was clutching the serving girl, grinning like an idiot. Everyone was watching him, waiting to see what he would do. Only two people seemed horrified by Gessler's suggestion: an elderly man and a woman sitting at the end, but the woman's hand was firmly gripping the man's arm, warning him not to intercede. Tell caught the eye of a young boy at the centre of the table. The boy looked away, embarrassed. Well, that made three of them. But three just wasn't enough.

'Well?' Gessler asked.

Tell nodded. He had no choice.

A black knight approached him and held out a weapon. Tell took it, weighing it with balanced hands. It felt like a part of him, something that had been missing for too long. This was a clumsy weapon. It was made of wood, not horn, and the sinew had been left in the rain. He had taken more care of his own weapon. But he would be given no choice. The black knight held out a quiver full of bolts. Tell took two. One he put in his belt. The other he loaded into the bow.

'You don't think I'm going to let you have a second shot, do you?' Gessler mocked, walking back to his chair.

Ignoring him, Tell lifted the crossbow.

And aimed.

The crossbow stretched out in front of him. His eyes focused on the apple. He was aiming too high. He lowered his left hand.

And looked into Matthew's eyes.

Matthew . . .

He had fired many times, sometimes to kill, sometimes to wound. He was known for his skill as a marksman, admired for it.

He never missed.

But this was his son.

His hand was trembling. If he trembled, he

would have no control. The bolt might go too high.

Or too low.

His son . . .

A son he loved . . .

Tell took a deep breath, forcing his hand to steady itself. Now it was perfect. The sights were square on the apple. His finger reached for the trigger.

'Take a step back.'

Gessler's voice shattered his concentration. His whole arm was taut, his finger hooked round the trigger. Slowly, he uncurled it again. He stepped back.

'And another.'

He stepped back.

'And another.'

One more step. Now he was twenty-five yards away. And the apple was smaller than ever.

'Now . . .'

Gessler fell silent again. Once more Tell lifted the crossbow, found the apple with the sights.

But this time he couldn't fire. Silently he screamed at his finger. But it wouldn't move.

Not at his son . . .

'Damn them, Father! Shoot!'

Matthew's words, defiant, unafraid, were like a torrent of cold water. They washed over Tell and a second later he fired.

The apple exploded.

Matthew groaned and fainted. Two wisps of hair remained pinned to the pole.

The Governor of Ursen looked away.

Prince Martin stared at Matthew.

Nobody spoke.

And then Tell reloaded the crossbow. The second bolt was already lying along the stock. He brought it round, sweeping the sights along the table, past the assorted guests. The tip of the bolt pointed at Gessler's heart.

But Tyrrol was behind him. Tyrrol had crept forward even as he aimed. His crossbow was raised above his head and before Tell could fire he brought it crashing down into the back of his neck.

Tell's knees buckled. He fell.

'You were right,' Prince Frederick muttered. 'He really is rather a good shot.'

Two: The Prisoner

The boat slid silently across the lake, enshrouded by a thick mist which swirled around its bows. It was a cold morning. The sun had barely risen above the horizon, struggling against the weight of the clouds that surrounded it. Not a sound could be heard. Even the chop of the waves had been smothered up in the gloom of the day. A single bird hovered over the boat, a black scrap of bone and feather, lost, endlessly circling.

William Tell stood on the deck, four chains leading from the collar that had been locked around his neck. If he felt the chill of the dawn or the still colder touch of fear, he did not show it. He stood like a statue, surrounded by the great silence, travelling ever further into the blankness of his own death.

But now a shape appeared, looming out of the mist on the opposite bank of the lake. It was a huge bulk of grey and black, rising out of the ground, its towers and turrets disappearing into the clouds. It was a castle, but from this distance it could have been a giant skull, its eyes two windows, its mouth and teeth a portcullis pulled open to receive him.

The boat reached a jetty where two armed soldiers stood waiting. Nobody spoke as the boat was made fast, the mildewed ropes tied to two iron rings. A black knight appeared on the deck. The chains were untied. Tell was led onto dry land.

The castle seemed even more horrible close to than it had from the lake. Its bricks looked as old as time itself, dripping with dew, snarled with fungi and weeds. There were twenty or more windows facing out over the water, all of them barred. Inside, the rooms – or cells – were black. The castle was giving no secrets away. Somewhere somebody screamed. Or perhaps it was the echo of a scream uttered centuries before.

'Death Castle.' Gessler had climbed out of the interior of the boat and was standing next to Tell, rubbing his hands against the cold. Unlike Tell, he was swathed in a thick cloak, a fox-fur collar around his neck. 'It's not the most original name, but I suppose it's apt enough.' He laughed to himself. 'Take a good look at it, Tell. You'll never see it from the outside again.'

A small, fat man had waddled out of the gate, his breath turning white in the cold. He had a face like a rotten peach, the cheeks puffed out and vaguely spherical, the skin wrinkled and, in places, pockmarked. Hair of no particular colour sprouted out of the back of his head, reaching down to his neck. Gessler smelt him before he saw him.

'Ah – Warden,' he muttered.

'My Lord . . .' The warden stopped to recover his breath. He was trembling from head to foot – and not just because of the cold. 'I would have been here to welcome you personally, my lord, but I was . . .'

'Not another word!' Gessler held up a hand and the warden stammered to a halt. 'I've brought you a prisoner who is going to require special handling. He's to be kept in a cell by himself, as far away from the other prisoners as possible.'

The warden's face fell. 'But my lord,' he whined, 'I have no more cells. We're over-crowded already and . . .'

'This is meant to be a death castle, not a hotel!' Gessler cut in. 'If you haven't got enough room, hang some prisoners and make some. I want this man to have a cell to himself. And you're to leave him there to rot . . . unless you feel the need to take him out and beat him. And if you decide to do that, make sure you get a mask.'

'I'm to wear a mask when I beat him?' the warden queried.

'No – *he* is, you idiot! I don't want his face seen. And I don't want any of the other prisoners to speak to him.' The warden was looking even unhappier than before, so Gessler added, 'Don't worry – he won't be here for long.'

'Ah!' The warden nodded appreciatively. 'Another gallows bird . . . What's his name?'

'He has no name,' Gessler said.

The warden signalled and Tell was led into the castle through the open portcullis. Inside was a large courtyard. In the distance, a line of prisoners was making its way towards an open field, as pitted with graves as the warden's face was with spots. Each man was chained to the other, the iron rings rubbing their ankles raw. They were carrying a wooden platform, two bodies lying limp on the top. As they shuffled forward, a guard lashed at them with a whip. It was an ugly sight, made uglier by the obvious pleasure it gave Gessler.

'I'll leave you here,' he said. 'Goodbye, Tell. We won't meet again.'

'Gessler!' The word was no more than a whisper, rasping in Tell's throat. 'What happened to my son?'

Gessler said nothing.

'Is he safe?'

Gessler sniffed. 'Of course he isn't safe. What makes you think he's even alive?'

'Damn you, Gessler!' Tell lunged forward, but the guards were already there, stepping in between him and the Governor. 'What do you want with me?'

Gessler considered the question. Then suddenly, unexpectedly he struck. The back of his hand lashed Tell's cheek, rocking him to one side. 'Listen to me, William Tell,' he said. 'You get no answers. You have no rights. You are nothing. Nothing! Do you understand?'

Tell brought his head up slowly, until his eyes were locked with Gessler's. He didn't speak. But his eyes said more than words ever could.

'You stay in this hole and you rot,' Gessler went on. 'One day, perhaps I will show you mercy. On that day you will die.'

Gessler turned round and walked away. Tell watched him go. The portcullis slid shut behind him.

Although he had tried not to show it, Gessler was a worried man. He had planned to create a symbol, something to impress the Emperor. With the apple and the crossbow he had created a symbol sure enough, but it was not quite the symbol he had had in mind.

All over the country people were talking about it . . . Gessler's cruelty, Matthew's defiance, Tell's courage. It was almost as if, in firing the bolt, Tell had taken the first shot at the very fabric of the Empire and by hitting his target had dealt what would one day be seen as its death blow. William Tell. All the stories about his past, his time as a mercenary, were being whispered abroad. It was said that Gessler was terrified of him, that Prince Frederick himself had fled from the province to get away from him. Brother Gregory had once said that the people were looking for a leader. It seemed that in William Tell they had found one.

Gessler had done what he could to staunch the flood of rumours and to deflate the legend that he had unwittingly created. His black knights put it about that Tell had missed his target, that he had killed his son. A body was produced and buried, well before anyone could see its face. William Tell was safely locked up in Death Castle, where he would stay and rot. Of Matthew himself there was no news whatsoever.

But despite all this, the story wouldn't go away. If anything, it grew stronger, more potent, as it was passed from mouth to mouth. In one village, a black knight was dragged off his horse and beaten within an inch of his life. All over the country, hats were being ripped off poles, thrown to the ground and trampled. Three months had passed since the banquet but it could have been three days. William Tell . . . William Tell . . . the name had become an inspiration. And rapidly, irresistibly, the people were beginning to unite behind it.

'I can't understand it!' Gessler exclaimed, as he sat pondering in the great hall of his castle. 'What is their interest in this man . . . this nobody?'

'I don't know.' Tyrrol was standing in front of him, his watery eyes filled with something that Gessler had never seen there before – something that might have been fear. 'But everywhere we go it's the same. They've heard what you made him do at the banquet. And they don't like it.'

'They'll forget about him soon enough.' Gessler pulled a leg off a roast chicken and waved it at Tyrrol. 'It just needs more time to blow over.' He ripped the flesh off the bone with his teeth and chewed silently for a moment. 'But perhaps we can hasten the progress a little. What was the name of Tell's village?'

'Clairmont.'

'Go there. Take two dozen men. Burn the place down.'

'Burn it?'

'Are you going deaf, Tyrrol?' Gessler threw the chicken leg onto the floor. A wolfhound lunged out from beneath a table and snapped it up. 'Do what I tell you. You say that Tell's name has come to mean freedom and independence? Well . . . let's see how often it's spoken when it comes to mean death!'

And so it was that death came to Clairmont.

Tyrrol and his men arrived later that day, riding out of the afternoon sun. There was no warning, no chance for anyone to prepare themselves. The black knights were carrying lit firebrands, the smoke trailing behind them. Their faces were hidden, covered by iron helmets with only slits for the eyes. They didn't speak. Nor did they hesitate. Like a plague of locusts they rode into the bustling village.

The next twenty minutes were a nightmare of billowing fire and clashing steel. Caught unawares, the villagers didn't even try to resist. And how could they fight – without weapons, without horses of their own? Screaming, running in all directions, they grabbed what few possessions they could carry and fled for the shelter of the woods. Not all of them made it. The unfortunate few who stood in the way of the black knights were cut down where they stood.

One after another the village houses went up in flames. Tell's workshop was the first to go, the wattle roof erupting in a mushroom of fire, the timbers crashing down onto the forge and bellows. Tyrrol had understood Gessler's orders only too well. The sun had risen that morning on a cheerful, thriving community. Now its rays were blotted out by a swirling blanket of smoke. Even the livestock, the chickens and goats, were snatched up and taken to be served at the next banquet. By the time Tyrrol gave the order to leave, it was as if the village had never existed.

Katrina was lucky. Fearing just such a reprisal, Brother Gregory had persuaded her to leave Clairmont for a place of safety. Even now he was with her, travelling south, and it would be many weeks before either of them heard what had happened. Roland and Blade also survived. They had fought with a courage that was blind to the odds. Blade had managed to knock one black knight from his horse and would have killed him if she hadn't been struck down from behind. Roland had come within an inch of killing Tyrrol himself, his bolt deflected by the side of Tyrrol's helmet. With seven other villagers, they were taken prisoner. The reward for their resistance would be a more lingering death.

As Tyrrol and the black knights rode back towards Gessler's castle, they left a smouldering ruin on the horizon behind them. The smoke, still rising into the air, would be seen for miles around. The wind would carry it across the country, and the whispers would go with it. Gessler had struck back. His cruelty had gone to new extremes. The village of Clairmont was no more.

William Tell opened his eyes. He could no longer tell whether it was night or day. There was no window in his tiny cell and the two had merged into a great, empty timelessness. How long had he been in Death Castle? He knew that it was more than a month, perhaps more than two. After seven weeks he had stopped even trying to keep count.

There was a clang of metal as a cell door was opened – a familiar sound in the depths of the prison block – and in the distance he heard someone shouting, a high-pitched, angry voice that reminded him of something or someone. He closed his eyes.

'You fools. You murdering fools . . .'

Now he remembered. The man in the tavern

where Matthew had once gone. Another time. Another world. The man must have offered some resistance for a moment later he was thrown across the corridor, crashing into the bars of Tell's prison. He opened his eyes and looked through the bars. At once he recognized the thin, bearded face and fanatical eyes of the young revolutionary, Roland.

'Clairmont . . .' he whispered, in a voice grown hoarse from starvation. 'What's happening?'

'They burnt it down, killed everyone . . .'

Roland got no further. 'You're not to talk to him!' The guard grabbed hold of the new prisoner and jerked him back, away from the cell. A door was opened and closed with the cold echo of steel. Footsteps pounded down the corridor. A second door boomed shut. Then silence.

Tell propped himself up against the stone wall, a wave of despair coursing through him. So it hadn't ended with him. 'They killed everyone.' Katrina. Brother Gregory.

He took a deep breath, clenching and unclenching his fist. It was time for action.

In a chamber on one of the upper levels of Death Castle, Gessler was thinking exactly the same thing. Despite everything he had done, the situation was steadily worsening. He had burnt down Clairmont. Three more villages had followed it. If he destroyed much more, he would have no province left. Without a province he would not be able to collect taxes. And without taxes it would not be long before he ended up a prisoner himself.

He had crossed the lake with one aim in mind. William Tell had started it. William Tell must die. Gessler was angry with himself. If he had hanged the man and produced the body three months ago, he might have deflated the legend before it could blow up out of all proportion – as it had now. But it still might not be too late.

'You have William Tell secure?' he demanded.

'Yes, my lord.' The warden smiled and ducked his head. 'He's more dead than alive, but . . .'

'Then kill him. Do it now. I want an end to the matter once and for all.'

'As you wish, my lord . . .'

There was one thing Gessler did not know.

The warden was a curious man. As the custodian of Death Castle, where as many as a dozen men might face the hangman in one day, he had become superstitious. How would he, who had judged so many, be judged when it was his turn to face death? Every morning he prayed in a small private chapel. And, in the hope that God might forgive him for his crimes, he employed a monk, a sickly, drunken man whose task it was to bless each and every one of the condemned prisoners before they were taken to the noose. It was as much as the warden could do, but it comforted him. If his prisoners could meet their maker in a state of grace, who knows but that they might have a kind word to say for him when he was finally called?

So that morning, the monk was sent once again into the cells to give absolution to William Tell. Two guards escorted him, unlocked the gate and then locked him in. Tell was lying on his side, seemingly asleep.

'My brother,' the monk began, as he had begun countless times before. 'Your time on earth is coming to an end.'

Tell stirred and rolled over.

'Make confession and prepare yourself for the last judgement.'

Tell opened his eyes.

'Do you want to pray with me?'

Tell's hand shot out. It was the last thing the monk remembered.

Ten minutes later the guards returned to the cell. Nobody had told them the identity of the man they were about to hang, but they didn't really care anyway. What did names matter in a place like Death Castle? Working there was like walking through a cemetery. The very sight of the stones told you where you were. Reading the epitaphs would tell you little more.

They reached the cell and looked in through the bars. The monk was still there, standing over the body of the prisoner which lay stretched out in the cell. He was mumbling in Latin, agitatedly, drawing the sign of the cross in the air.

'All right, Father,' one of the guards muttered

as he unlocked the door. 'You'll have to save your amens for later.'

The monk turned round. The guard just had time to register that it wasn't the monk. But he didn't have time to call out. Tell's fist caught him square on the jaw, knocking him out. The second guard backed away. Tell lunged at him, hurling him into a brazier that burnt on the opposite side of the passage. The guard just managed to miss the flames. Instead he hit the wall with an audible 'crack'. He slithered to the ground and lay still.

Tell snatched the key out of the lock. There was only one key on the chain. It would open every cell door. Already the other prisoners were yelling at him, pleading with him to release them, recognizing there would never be another chance. Tell hesitated. He had to get out while there was still time, before the shouting aroused the other guards. But he couldn't leave the others behind. Hastily he pulled off the robe that he had taken from the monk. Then he ran towards the nearest door.

But he didn't have time to unlock it. Alerted by the noise, six more guards suddenly burst into the corridor. Tell was unarmed. They carried crossbows. For an agonizing second he found himself staring into the eyes of Roland. The woman – Blade – was crouched behind him. Both of them were pleading soundlessly with him: open the door, don't leave us here. He glanced down the corridor. The flames from the brazier were spreading, devouring the straw on the ground and the wooden beams that supported the walls. Right now they were a barrier between him and the guards. Soon they would kill everyone in the cells.

But he had no time. The first guards broke through. Tell turned and ran, taking the key with him.

'You can't leave us here!' Roland's voice was a scream of fear and desperation. 'The key!'

He was too late. Tell had already gone. Plunging through the smoke and flames, the guards ran after him. Somewhere in the castle, a warning bell began to chime.

Gessler heard it.

'What is it?' he demanded, seizing hold of the cowering warden. 'What does it mean?'

'It's . . . an escape.' The warden swallowed, hardly daring utter the word.

'An escape?' Gessler was white-faced. He moved towards the door. 'Tell . . . !'

William Tell climbed a staircase. He had no idea where he was going. Only the knowledge of what he was escaping from gave him new strength. If it hadn't been for Roland and his news of Tell's village, he might never have attempted this. He was outnumbered a hundred to one. But Clairmont had been burnt. Katrina had been there. He had to find her. He had to find Matthew.

A guard turned a corner at the top of the

staircase, his crossbow at the ready. Tell ducked. The bolt whistled over his shoulder, finding its target in the heart of the guard who was leading the pursuit behind him. Tell lunged forward. The guard doubled up. Tell snatched his crossbow, then reached down for a bolt. When at last he reached the daylight and found himself out in the open courtyard, he was armed.

He ran forward. Somewhere in the back of his mind he was adding up the possibilities. He remembered the portcullis. That would surely have been lowered once the alarm was raised. And even if he could get through it, he was utterly surrounded by water. The boat might be there, but it would be guarded. He could not go out. He could not go back. That only left up.

A bolt struck the brickwork beside his head, a wooden splinter ricocheting into his neck. The guards were close behind him. Twenty more of them were running across the courtyard towards him. There was a staircase set into the wall. He took it, his shoulders rasping against the rough stone as he spiralled upward.

The staircase led to the battlements. There was another guard waiting for him at the top. Tell could have shot him, but he had only one bolt and that would have left him unarmed once again. Ducking, he charged like a bull. The guard swept at him with a sword. Tell's head made contact with his stomach. The guard grunted, then yelled out as Tell heaved upwards, spinning him over his head. The guard plummeted back down the stairs. Tell smiled grimly to himself as he heard the falling body crash into the other guards who were following him. He still had his bolt.

And then he found Gessler.

Gessler had taken up his sword and rushed out of the warden's office as soon as he heard the bell. The office was in the south tower, overlooking the lake. He had hurried across the battlements towards the prison block even as Tell had broken into the daylight. And now the two men stood facing each other, only ten yards apart. Tell had his crossbow and the bolt. Gessler had only a sword.

'Tell . . .'

A feeling of hatred welled up inside Tell, stronger than anything he had ever felt. This man had destroyed him. Even if he escaped from the castle, his life would never be the same again. His wife might be dead. His son was missing. His home had been destroyed. For years he had ignored Gessler's tyranny. For years he had fooled himself that it had nothing to do with him. And then, because of a whim, a pathetic gesture for a visiting prince, he had become Gessler's victim. He remembered the apple, remembered Matthew's face through the sights of a crossbow. William Tell had never killed in anger. But he would kill Gessler now. He should have killed him years before.

The soldiers had reached the battlements, but nobody moved. There were a dozen of them behind him, a dozen more ahead. To one side, a small, semi-circular terrace stretched out over the lake with a drop of several hundred feet to the grey surface of the water. The acrid tang of smoke hung in the air, carried by the breeze. Tell remembered the fire in the prison. But his thoughts were only on Gessler.

'Let me live,' Gessler whispered. There was sweat on his forehead. An inch at a time he edged towards Tell. 'I promise you – you can go free. Your son . . .'

'Where is he, Gessler?' Tell demanded.

'I'll tell you . . . everything you want to know . . .'

Gessler was moving closer by the second. He was still holding his sword. Soon he would be within striking distance. And the soldiers too were closing in.

'Tell . . .'

The voice came from the distance, from the far corner of the courtyard.

'Help us!'

Tell glanced out of the corner of his eye. There was an iron grate, at ground level. Smoke was billowing out of it and he could also make out the red glow of flames. There was a figure trapped there, his arms stretching out, beseeching.

Roland. He was being burnt alive. And Tell had the key.

'Gessler . . .' Tell hissed, backing onto the terrace, his crossbow still aimed at the Governor.

Gessler looked up. Their eyes locked. It was what Tell had been hoping for. With his attention misdirected, Tell slid the key out of his pocket and looped it onto the bolt.

'Where is Matthew?'

Gessler said nothing. It was too late. Tell couldn't wait any longer. He spun round and fired. The grate was small and far away. Roland's body blocked most of it. But Tell had found the tiny space that was left. The bolt sped across the courtyard taking the key with it. It went over Roland's shoulder, struck one of the cell walls.

Roland had the key. But Tell was defenceless.

'That's it, Tell,' Gessler said.

Tell turned round and jumped.

His feet left the terrace and he soared over the castle battlements. In mid-air he jackknifed round and into a diving position. Three guards fired at him, but he had taken them by surprise. He was moving too fast. Down he plummeted. Down, down, down . . . his arms stretching out for the water. Then he hit the lake, knifing through the surface and disappearing into the depths. Gessler ran forward to the edge of the castle and looked down. There was no sign of Tell. Only a spiralling ring showed where he had dived.

The warden had seen it all. Puffing with the exertion of the climb, he leant over the battlement and peered at the lake. The ripples smoothed themselves out and disappeared. There were no air bubbles.

'He couldn't have survived,' the warden muttered. 'No one could have survived. He's dead. He has to be.'

'No.' Gessler shook his head, his eyes dark with fury. 'William Tell isn't dead. He's out there. He's alive . . . and he's free!'

Three: The Search

Two men were strolling beside the lake. One walked with a spring in his step, his eyes twinkling and a wicked smile on his face. He was a man who had never quite stopped being a boy. His name was Ambrose. The other man slouched behind him. Pale and plump, with thinning hair and thickening stomach, he was remarkable only in that he had no chin. People called him Weevil, although that was surely not the name he had been christened with.

The two of them were arguing. They were always arguing. Usually about money. Money was something they usually didn't have.

'Are you seriously telling me, Weevil, that you sold your knife for a chicken?'

'It's a very nice chicken, Ambrose,' Weevil said.

The chicken squawked as if in agreement. Ambrose sighed.

'Fine, Weevil. Fine,' he said. 'But how can you hope to be a successful criminal armed only with a chicken? I mean, when it comes to robbing someone, what are you going to do? Hit them with a drumstick?'

'I don't want to hit anyone, Ambrose.'

'Sssh!'

Ambrose held up a hand. He had seen someone, a man, sitting slumped against a tree, his clothes drying in the sun. Ambrose was stupid. But he wasn't quite as stupid as Weevil. The man had to be a prisoner, escaped from Death Castle. Why else would he have swum across the lake?

'Looks like a drowned rat,' Weevil whispered.

'Must have chewed his way out of the castle,' Ambrose said. His eyes lit up. 'How much do you think it'd be worth to take him back?'

'A couple of pennies?' Weevil suggested.

'Basic economics, Weevil!' This was Ambrose's favourite expression, although he wasn't quite sure what it meant. 'There's bound to be a reward out for him – and more than a few pennies. All we have to do is take him.'

'You're going to take him?' Weevil asked.

Ambrose looked at the silent man. He looked exhausted. But he also looked strong. He swallowed. 'No,' he said. He took the chicken and gave Weevil his knife. 'You take him.'

Weevil smiled weakly. Lacking a chin, it was difficult to smile in any other way. Then he tiptoed forward, clasping the knife. Tell's eyes flickered open.

'You're . . .' Weevil began.

That was as far as he got. He had woken a sleeping tiger. A foot shot out, driving all the wind out of his body. He dropped the knife. The man caught it and sliced upwards in one movement. Weevil shrieked as his shirt fell into two pieces. Then he turned and ran. Ambrose had already gone. At the first sign of trouble he had taken off like a rabbit. The chicken followed.

Tell got to his feet. He had slept for longer than he had meant to. The sun was high in the sky and he had no doubt that Gessler would have already sent his soldiers after him. Apart from the knife he had just been given, he was unarmed. Worse still, after three months in Death Castle he was close to starvation and his escape had drained away what little strength he had left. He had tried eating an apple plucked from a tree, but it was sour. If he didn't eat soon, he would die. He turned away from the lake and began to walk, plunging into the thick forest land surrounding him, grateful for its cover.

He walked for an hour. Then the world began to spin and he had to rest, leaning against a tree. The air was warm and scented and his clothes had dried at least. And so far he hadn't been followed.

There was a faint crack as a twig snapped and suddenly Tell was fully alert once again. He didn't move but he searched the forest with his ears and the corners of his eyes. There was a rustle of leaves. Someone was watching him, moving closer through the undergrowth. He took a few steps forward then ducked to one side, disappearing behind the thick trunk of a tree.

Edging round, his back against the bark, he looked the way he had come. A figure pressed forward through a clump of bushes. It was holding a crossbow. Tell acted.

He grabbed the crossbow and pulled it forward. At the same time he struck out with his fist. There was a high-pitched yell and the figure fell back, its shoulders hitting the ground. Tell looked down and sighed. He had just knocked out a boy, a ten-year-old boy. The crossbow hadn't even been loaded.

The warden stared down at the ground which his feet no longer touched with eyes that no longer saw. The thick rope around his neck creaked in the afternoon breeze and his body swung gently in a small circle.

Gessler had hanged him at noon. Gessler wished he had hanged him six months ago. Eight people had escaped from Death Castle that day. Roland and Blade had been among them, breaking through the portcullis and overpowering the guards at the boat. The fact that they were free hardly mattered. They could be hunted down in good time. But the news would escape with them. They had been in Death Castle and they had lived. It was another crack in the iron wall of Gessler's rule. The people would hear. The people would be a little less afraid.

And Tell had escaped with them. Tell and the apple. That worried Gessler more. He looked past the hanging warden at the ruin of the castle. It looked as if a war had taken place. One wing was still on fire. The bodies of the guards lay heaped in a corner, waiting for burial. And the memory of Tell's incredible dive to freedom still lingered in the minds of those who had survived. They were whispering amongst themselves and, as Gessler crossed the castle courtyard, they avoided his eyes. Nobody had said it but they knew all the same. In William Tell, Gessler had finally met his match. Every moment that he was alive, Gessler's power would be weakened. It was the beginning of the end.

'Tyrrol!'

The commander of the black knights snapped to attention. There were thirty men waiting behind him in the courtyard, waiting for Gessler's orders.

'You're ready?' Gessler demanded.

'Yes, my lord.'

'Track him down, Tyrrol. Search the land. If anybody gets in your way, kill them. But don't kill Tell. Bring him to me alive.'

'Alive, my lord?' Tyrrol scowled in puzzlement.

'Alive!' Gessler spun on his heels. 'I can't hang a dead man.'

William Tell carried the boy out of the forest and down a gentle slope into a small farming community. From the distance, the farm had looked beautiful, a miniature haven of peace and civilization in a land that had for too long been steeped in blood. But closer to, he saw that it had not escaped Gessler's tyranny. It had happened perhaps a month ago. The buildings had been set on fire, most of them destroyed. Two of them were missing their roofs. Crumbling brickwork, broken beams and splinters of smashed pottery lay strewn around the grass which was already choked up with weeds.

Only one of the buildings, a small cottage, remained intact. As Tell walked forward a door opened and a woman ran out. She had been working in the garden and still carried a hoe – but now she grasped it like a spear, the sharp metal head pointing at Tell.

'Who are you?' she demanded. 'What have you done to Simon?'

'Simon?' Tell looked at the boy and laid him gently on the ground. 'He'll be all right,' he said. 'I knocked him out.'

'Why? He's only a boy.'

'Maybe. But he was tracking me in the forest. He had a crossbow . . .'

The boy was still clutching the crossbow, evidence of the truth of Tell's words. Seeing it, the woman lowered the hoe and sighed. 'Simon,' she said. 'I told you . . .'

'I was playing,' The boy stood up.

'That sort of playing could get you killed,' Tell said, mildly.

The woman ran forward and examined her son. There was a bruise on his cheek but nothing more serious than that. At the same time, Tell examined her. Like the boy, she had fair hair and blue eyes, a pale face and narrow, tight-set lips. They had something more in common, something that went beyond physical appearances. They had seen something, lived through some terrible experience, and it had left its scars on both of them.

'Thank you for bringing him here,' the woman said. 'I don't have much to give you, but if you need food . . .'

'I haven't eaten for days,' Tell said.

'Then come into the house. My name is Isabel . . .'

The house was small. Like Tell's own home in Clairmont it had only one room that doubled as a living and a sleeping area. But Isabel had made it as comfortable as possible, decorating it with wild flowers in hand-painted pottery vases that seemed to belong to another time, a time before Gessler and his black knights.

She cooked a meal and Tell ate ravenously. Simon sat next to him, eating nothing, not even opening his mouth to speak. He was only ten, but the hatred that emanated from him was entirely adult and took away his youth, turning him into an old man. As Tell finished, Isabel told him her story. Her voice was soft, emotionless. She was like the victim of a city that has been hit by an earthquake. There had been so much horror, so much suffering, that her own tragedy had become almost commonplace.

She had lived in the farm with her husband and with two other couples and their families. While the others had tended the land and looked after the animals, her husband had worked at the kiln, crafting pots which he would sell in the local market. The three families would share the profits which they used to buy seeds or farming equipment. They had all worked long hours, rising and going to bed with the sun. But they had enough to eat. They had each other. And in their own simple way they were happy.

Then a black knight had been killed by rebels in a nearby village. His body had been discovered. Gessler had decided to take revenge. The true killers couldn't be found – so an example had been made.

'My husband was sitting where you are now,' Isabel said. 'The soldiers rode in and we heard the screaming outside. It all happened so fast. We thought they wouldn't do anything to us – just frighten us, maybe take some food. There wasn't anything we could do. There was a jug of flowers on the table. One of the soldiers smashed it with his sword. I remember thinking it was such a stupid thing to do. So unnecessary. And then . . .'

'They killed him.' These were the first words Simon had spoken.

'They killed all the men,' Isabel went on. 'The women and the children were left alone. The other families left after a time. Simon and I have been alone here for a month now. We still have the land, but . . .'

Her voice trailed away and there were tears in her eyes. Simon was staring at his mother, his face set in an almost animal snarl. Then he pounded his fist on the table, got up and ran out of the room.

'I'm sorry.' Isabel wiped her eyes. 'He worshipped his father. But John was a potter – not a fighter.'

'Whose crossbow is it?' Tell gestured at the crossbow. Simon had brought it in with him and set it down beside the table while they ate. Tell suspected that the boy carried it everywhere.

'I don't know where he found it,' Isabel said. 'He doesn't even know how to use it. I suppose that's one thing to be grateful for. One day he'll get himself killed.'

Tell thought for a moment. Then he got up and took the crossbow.

'What are you doing?' Isabel asked.

'Wait here.'

Simon was sitting on the stump of a dead tree just outside the farm, fiddling with a bolt that presumably belonged to the crossbow. Softly, Tell approached and sat down beside him.

'Simon?' he said.

'Yes . . . ?'

'I brought you this.' He lowered the crossbow.

'What of it?'

'Your mother tells me you don't know how to use it. I can show you.'

For the first time Simon glanced at Tell with a faint stirring of interest. Tell had never seen a boy so eaten up by hatred. It had entered his bloodstream like a poison, worked its way through every fibre of his being. Tell knew what such hatred could do. When he had stood in front of Gessler in the courtyard of Death Castle, he had seen the same hatred and suffered its consequences. Simon was no Gessler. But left to himself, he could all too easily grow into one.

'It's a good crossbow.' Tell lowered it so that he could place his foot in the stirrup underneath the bridle. With practised ease he pulled the bow-string back and hooked it over the tiller. He reached out for the bolt and Simon gave it to him. When he stood up a moment later, the crossbow was armed and ready. 'You want to fire it?'

Simon nodded and stood next to Tell. A barn door rested against a tree about twenty yards away. The barn itself had been burnt to the ground at the time of the soldiers' attack. 'That's your target,' Tell said.

Simon aimed. His whole body was taut now, as taut as the bow-string itself. Tell wondered what he was imagining as he aimed down the sights. The barn door was an easy target, old and warped. But to Simon it would be a soldier, maybe Gessler himself, a man to be killed.

'Relax,' Tell advised him. 'If you don't relax, you won't have any control when you fire. That's better. Now . . . pull the trigger gently. Aim for the very centre . . .'

Simon fired.

His aim was wild, the bolt slamming into one side of the door, close to the edge. At the same time, the boy reeled backwards, surprised by the force of the shot. He stood in silence for a moment, then lowered it. Tell wasn't surprised to see that he was trembling. When he had picked up the crossbow, he had thought of it as no more than a toy. Now he was beginning to learn that it was in reality a deadly weapon.

Tell walked over to the barn door and took hold of the bolt. He pulled it with all his strength and slowly it came free, tearing the wood with a sickening crunch.

'If this had been a man, the bolt would have crippled or killed him,' Tell explained. 'You've been carrying that crossbow round like a toy – but you don't understand. It's a weapon. A very nasty weapon. The crossbow is five times more powerful than the ordinary bow. I've seen a bolt go right through a man, in one side and out the other. Do you really think you could fire at a man, Simon?'

Simon stared at the wreckage of the door and said nothing. Tell handed him the bolt. 'Killing never solves anything. Once you start killing you go on killing until one day you're killed yourself.' Without realizing he was doing it, Simon had begun to cry. Tell patted him gently on the shoulder. 'There are other ways to fight back,' he said. 'And it's time you and I got started.'

Two miles away from the farm, between the lake and a forest, Roland was also holding a crossbow – not with hatred but with raw determination. He was surrounded by six ragged men and one woman. All of them were armed. The boat that they had stolen from Death Castle had turned out to be a floating arsenal. Blade was, as ever, at his side, the usual collection of knives poking out of every fold of her clothing. It wasn't quite an army. But it could be the beginnings of an army. Roland was an outlaw now. He would be hunted down until he dropped, and once he was found he would be hanged. The time for talking was over. Now he had to fight.

'William Tell . . .' he said.

'Tell?' Blade asked.

'He got us out.'

'And you want to thank him?'

'I want to use him.' Roland slammed the crossbow down. 'Look at us, Blade,' he cried. 'Eight of us. What can eight of us do against an Empire? If we're ever to be free, if we're ever going to beat Gessler, we've got to get the people behind us. But the people need a symbol . . . a figurehead.'

'But why Tell?' Blade demanded. 'Why not you?'

Roland smiled grimly. 'Because I didn't shoot an apple off a boy's head.' He got to his feet. 'Tell can't be far from here. So we'll start now. Every village, every farm . . .'

'And what if the black knights find us first?' Blade said.

'They won't be looking for us. Not until they've found Tell. And we've got to be sure *we* find him first.'

Tyrrol and the black knights had already crossed the lake and were riding slowly through the forest, pausing to examine the ground for signs of footprints, scraps of clothing or anything that might lead them to Tell. Night was already approaching and soon they would have to set up camp. It was unfortunate for Ambrose and Weevil that they chose this moment to appear.

The two rogues had barely recovered from their failed assault on Tell. Weevil was sulking. His shirt was hanging off him in two pieces and he had lost his chicken. He had been looking forward to that chicken all day. It was the only meat he had had to eat in a fortnight. As usual, Ambrose was optimistic. He was always planning something and seemed oblivious to the fact that his plans never, ever worked.

'Basic economics,' he was saying as they

trudged through the forest. 'The "returned prisoner" market may not be booming at the moment. But what about highway robbery?'

'Highway robbery?' Weevil stared around him. 'But there aren't any highways, Ambrose.'

'Highways, low ways, anyways there's a killing to be made . . .'

'But whose killing?' Weevil whimpered.

'You worry too much,' Ambrose said. 'You'll see. We'll be rich before the sun sets. We'll rob the very next people who came along.'

'The very next people, Ambrose?'

'The very next people, Weevil.'

The very next people had already appeared, riding towards them. Weevil looked up and winced. But it was already too late to hide. And anyway, Ambrose had other ideas. 'Leave this to me,' he whispered.

Tyrrol reined in his horse and stared down at the two peasants. 'I'm looking for a man,' he said. 'Tall, brown hair, well-built. Have you seen him?'

'I might have,' Ambrose said with a sly smile, and Weevil shivered. 'But first, my lord, I wonder if there might be a reward for information received?'

'A reward?' Tyrrol would have laughed if Tyrrol ever laughed. Instead, he stared at Ambrose with murder in his eyes.

'Ambrose . . .' Weevil muttered.

But he was too late. 'Take them!' Tyrrol snapped out. At once, four black knights dismounted. 'Hang them upside-down. Whip them. Then ask them again.'

In the next twenty minutes, Ambrose learnt something about basic economics – and that was that they were basically useless when you were dealing with a black knight. And when Tyrrol asked him again, he babbled out the entire story of his meeting with Tell.

'It was north of here,' he moaned.

'North-west,' Weevil groaned.

'Yes. North and west. On the shore of the lake. There's a farm there.'

'Not far from there.'

'No. Very near there. That's where he'll have gone.'

'You should have told me when I asked you the first time,' Tyrrol said.

A moment later he was back on his horse and riding away with the thirty black knights behind him. Weevil wept tears of sheer relief. And even Ambrose would have gone on his knees and thanked the lord that they were still alive but for the fact that it was difficult to kneel and pray when he was still hanging upside-down from an oak, securely tied by the ankles.

Twenty-four hours had passed since Tell had arrived at the farm, but in that time he had transformed it. With Isabel he had examined the ruins of her husband's forge and then surprised her by rebuilding it, brick by brick.

'It wasn't as bad as it looked,' he had said.

'But the bellows . . .' Isabel pointed at the broken pieces of wood that had once fed the furnace that heated the kiln.

'I used to be a blacksmith,' Tell told her. 'I've mended worse than that.'

And Tell had been as true as his word. During his second day at the farm he mended the bellows and lit the fire. Simon hardly ever left his side, carrying wood, mixing clay, hammering nails and generally working with a glow of pure pleasure. To Isabel it was as if her son had come home to her after a long stay abroad. Since his lesson with the crossbow, he had changed. Instead of being eaten up by anger, he was using it. It was surging through him, lending him its strength. The farm would be rebuilt. He and his mother would live happily again. And for the black knights that would be the ultimate defeat.

Isabel looked wistfully at the man who had given them their life back again. She had shaved him and given him fresh clothes. They had eaten together, talked together, laughed together. But she still knew nothing about him. He hadn't even told her his name.

'I don't know how to thank you,' she said as she poured him a cup of cold water.

'Then don't try.'

'You've done so much for us. You know . . . if you wanted to . . . you could stay here. You're almost like a father to Simon. And I . . .'

Tell shook his head. 'You're kind. But soon I'll have to go. I have a wife of my own. And a son . . .'

'Mother! Soldiers!'

Simon ran into the farmhouse, his eyes wide with fear. Isabel looked nervously at Tell. Were they looking for him? What would they do if they found him there? It was as if he had read her mind. 'Stay in the house,' he said. 'It's me they want. They'll leave you alone once they've got me.'

Simon's crossbow was lying on the table with the bolt that he had fired into the barn door. Tell picked it up.

'What are you going to do?' Simon asked.

'Just stay with your mother. I'm going to give them what they want.'

Tell left the farmhouse.

Ironically, it had been the smoke from the kiln that had drawn Tyrrol and the black knights to the farmhouse. Now they moved forward in battle formation, Tyrrol in the vanguard, the thirty riders spreading out like an arrowhead behind him. Tell walked into the courtyard and faced them. The scattered buildings of the farming community stood on either side of him. In between, there was a long, narrow space. He was at one end. Tyrrol was at the other. There were a hundred yards between them.

Tyrrol smiled. He had expected Tell to be lying in wait, perhaps on one of the rooftops. But he had come out into the open, a lamb to the slaughter . . . only Gessler had said there was to be no killing. Very well. Tell would live. But whoever had been concealing him on the farm would die. Tyrrol would see that they died slowly. And Tell would watch.

'Forward!' he commanded.

But the black knights didn't move. The single man stood facing them, his crossbow hanging down towards the ground. Just one man against thirty! And for the first time, Tyrrol felt uneasy. There was something emanating from him, a feeling of power that was almost physical. It was incredible. There was no contest. No fight. So why were his men afraid?

'Forward!' he shouted again, spurring on his own horse to bear down on his opponent.

Tell raised his crossbow.

The black knights charged.

And almost at once seven of them fell to the ground. Tyrrol twisted round in his saddle even as he thundered down the passage. They had been shot at the same moment he had given the command. It had all happened so quickly that he hadn't even been able to see where the bolts had come from. And now Tell had vanished, ducking behind one of the ruined barns. What was happening? Who was the hidden enemy?

Tell had been equally surprised by the sudden onslaught. He had been ready to die. By sacrificing himself, he had hoped to save Isabel and

Simon, but now, at the last moment, the tables were turned. There was another volley of shots and three more soldiers were sent sprawling from their horses. It was the last thing he could have expected. But who . . . ?

Roland reloaded his bow and took careful aim. He and his men had arrived at the farm only minutes ahead of Tyrrol and had just had time to hide before the soldiers rode forward. As things had worked out, he was perfectly positioned, perched high up on the roof. The black knights were trapped on both sides. Beside him, Blade stood up, a knife in her hand. She spun it, caught the blade in her palm and threw. Another knight fell, reducing the odds still further.

But by now some of the knights had broken through the ambush. One of them caught up with Tell, his sword raised to finish it there and then, Gessler's orders forgotten. Tell twisted round, firing at the same time. The knight screamed and lurched out of his saddle, dropping the sword. Tell snatched it up, then lunged at the second rider who had charged from behind him. This time he only wounded the man, but for a few seconds the ground was clear. That was enough time for Tell. A bolt thudded into the wall beside him. He plucked it out, reloaded his bow in three seconds, searched for his next target.

'Tell!'

Tell froze. Tyrrol was sitting on his horse at the far end of the farm, away from the main area of fighting. His men were finished. Roland and his miniature army had seen to that. But Tyrrol wouldn't give up. He would take Tell back to Gessler or die in the attempt. And now he had the advantage. He had Simon.

Simon had broken free of his mother and run out into the yard almost as soon as the fighting began. He wanted to be part of it. It was his farm, his mother. He remembered the time when the black knights had come before, how the farmers had been almost too afraid to fight back. Their fear had killed them. But Simon wasn't afraid. If he had to die, he would die like a soldier, not like a slave.

Tyrrol had snatched him up as he galloped forward towards Tell. The boy weighed practically nothing. Tyrrol had swept him off his feet and now held him, pinned by one arm across his saddle, a knife at his throat. And now he was smiling. So long as he had the boy, there was nothing Tell could do . . . nothing he would dare to. Tyrrol might have lost the contest but he could still win the prize.

'Tell!' he shouted again. 'Drop your weapon. Surrender to me – or the boy dies!'

Tell looked past Tyrrol. He could see Roland now, standing on a roof top, urging his men on. The fighting was almost over, but they were too far away. By the time they saw what was happening at this end of the farm, Simon would be dead. And it would be Tell, not Tyrrol, who had killed him.

'Drop the crossbow, Tell! Do it now!'

Tyrrol was using Simon as a human shield. If Tell fired he would have more chance of hitting the boy than the knight. If he fired and wounded Tyrrol, then Simon would die anyway, his throat cut. He had only one chance. Shoot to kill. But how? There was only one part of the knight that was unprotected, an area of his neck just above Simon's head. Tell could see the circle of the flesh, but it was tiny . . .

The size of an apple.

He fired the crossbow. A wave of horror swept through him. He had missed. The bolt had hit Simon. But then Simon slid out of the saddle and sprawled on the ground and he saw that it was a trick of the light. Tyrrol screamed, a dreadful gurgling sound, the bolt stuck high in his chest. Then he went limp. The horse bolted forward and Tyrrol fell backwards, his feet tangled up in the stirrups. The horse galloped out of the farm, dragging the commander of the black knights behind it. Simon got weakly to his feet. Isabel rushed towards him and embraced him. Everything was suddenly silent in the farm. The fighting was over.

'Do you have to go?' Isabel asked.

Tell nodded.

'Simon's gone out to get more firewood. He'll want to say goodbye.'

'No.' Tell sighed. He couldn't explain what he was feeling to Isabel. He had saved Simon's life. But at the same time he had spoiled everything he had taught him. 'Killing never solves anything,' he had said. But in the end killing had been the only answer.

But Isabel understood, even without being told. 'You'll always be welcome here,' she said. 'If you ever want to come back . . .'

Tell walked out of the farmhouse. Outside, Roland and Blade were waiting for him. They had horses now, stolen from the black knights they had killed. Not one of the escaped prisoners had been hurt in the fight.

'Are you going to ride with us, Tell?' Roland demanded.

Tell stood beside the door, saying nothing.

'We saved you, Tell,' Roland went on. 'You owe us.'

'I owe you nothing, Roland.' Tell had chosen a horse for himself and now he got into the saddle. 'We're even. That's all.'

Roland walked forward. 'You can ride away from me, Tell. You can bury yourself in the forest, hide in the mountains. But you can't hide from what you are. You know it. And I know it. One day you'll fight with us and the whole country will fight behind you.'

Tell said nothing. Instead, he spurred his horse

and rode out of the farm, into the evening shadows.

'You'll be back, Tell!' Roland shouted.

But Tell had not heard him . . . or if he had, ignored him. A moment later he was gone, taken by the darkness which fell as a curtain behind him.

Four: The Stallion

The mountain ridges soared high above him, a jagged wall against the darkening sky. William Tell walked forward slowly, a tiny figure in the grim majesty of his surroundings. He had walked ten miles that day, his footsteps taking him ever further into a wilderness that seemed empty of any life other than the occasional goat that tugged at the grass on the rocky slopes. He had not seen a house or a farm since that morning, but even so, he knew that he was not alone. He was being watched, and had been for the past hour. He stopped for a moment, resting on the quarterstaff that he had cut from a tree. Where were they? When would they make their move?

As if in answer to his question, a man appeared, stepping out from behind a black outcrop. The man was dressed in rough leather trousers and a sheepskin jacket, belted at the waist. He was well over six foot tall, bearded, his face toughened by the mountain winds. He was older than Tell and stronger. He was also carrying a quarterstaff, tossing it from palm to palm. Tell looked around him. He was on a narrow path with a steep drop to one side. If he wanted to go forward he would have to pass the man.

He took a step towards him. The quarterstaff flashed and suddenly it was being held in both hands, pointing at Tell. The man hadn't spoken a word and his face hadn't changed, but his meaning was clear. If you want to go past, you have to fight me.

Tell lunged forward, hoping to take the man by surprise. But for someone so big, he was astonishingly fast. He didn't move so much as ripple and Tell's quarterstaff struck only air. At the same time, the man swung his own weapon round and Tell was almost thrown off the path as it thudded into his chest, winding him. Thrusting out to protect himself, he reeled back, then swung round again. The man parried three times, spun in a complete circle, hooked his quarterstaff behind Tell's and flicked upwards. Tell's weapon was plucked out of his hands. Even as he reached out for it he saw the man rotate his quarterstaff. The end pounded into his stomach. Tell sank to his knees.

The man looked at him and smiled. 'William Tell!' he cried. 'I didn't think we'd see you again.'

'Stefan . . .' Tell got weakly to his feet.

'You're still hopeless with the quarterstaff. Have you forgotten everything I taught you?'

'How could I?' Tell cradled his stomach. 'I've still got the bruises.'

'And well-deserved . . .'

Tell had only just got his breath back. But now Stefan moved forward and took him in a bear-like embrace that promptly drove it all out again. He glanced over the big man's shoulder and saw that another half-dozen men had left their hiding-places and appeared on the path. They were similarly dressed, the sheepskins vital protection against the freezing nights. One of them was looking at him with a scowl of displeasure. Tell vaguely remembered him – the blonde, wiry hair, the lip twisted into a permanent sneer – Morgan.

Stefan released him and slapped a hand down onto his shoulders with such force that he was almost sent flying again. 'We hear the news, even up here,' he said. 'When you left us, you were going back to the forge. You weren't going to fight any more. That's what you said . . .'

'We all make mistakes,' Tell muttered.

'And yours was leaving. I told you that at the time. There can never be any peace – not for people like you.'

'And what about you, Stefan?' Tell asked. 'You're still fighting?'

'What else can we do?' Stefan sighed and for a moment Tell saw pain in his eyes, a yearning for something passed or for something that could never be. 'We're wanted men – outlaws – all of us. Our faces are too well-known.' He shook his head. 'There can't be any going back.'

They moved on together, following the winding path ever further into the mountains. Soon they were surrounded by stone, towering up on all sides, blotting out all but the thinnest beams of light. Here everything was a silvery-grey: the rocks, the wild grass, the very clouds themselves seemed to have been painted with the same brush. It was a grim, desolate picture. Stefan and his men weren't just hiding from the Emperor. They were hiding from the world.

Just when it seemed that they could go no further, their path hemmed in on all sides, the rockface split open and there, perched on the slope that commanded the pass, Tell saw Stefan's hide-out. It was a castle. Once it would have been an impassable barrier for anyone trying to bring their armies across the mountains. But time – and some long-forgotten war – had humbled it. Two of its walls had been brought down. Makeshift huts leant for shelter against the walls that were left. Its courtyards were exposed, the weeds running wild over the brickwork, the wind sweeping in and out of the chinks. Two towers remained standing. A third had crumbled away. It was the sort of ruin that looks as if it was a ruin the day it was built, the sort of ruin that could not have been anything else.

'Remember it, William?'

Tell nodded. As a young man, when he had left his parents' home to become a mercenary, he had somehow found his way to Stefan's fortress. For three years he had fought with Stefan and his men, but first he had been taught how to fight

. . . with the sword, the quarterstaff and the slingshot. Stefan had wanted to teach him how to use the crossbow too, but, as Tell had quickly demonstrated, there had been no need. He had been handling the weapon almost from the time he first learnt to walk and his incredible accuracy had made him the admiration of everyone in the camp – with the single exception of Morgan, who had envied and resented him from the start.

Morgan was walking with the other men, following Stefan to the camp. As he walked he spoke in a soft, persuasive voice. Morgan had his own following in the camp. Stefan was getting old. They were going nowhere. A new future meant a new leader. Morgan was ready to lead.

'William Tell,' he said. 'We can use him.'

'How?' The questioner was a short man with curly hair and hollow eyes. His chin was covered with uneven stubble and angry red pockmarks.

'He could be our chance . . . our way out.'

'What are you saying, Morgan?' A wizened man with a pointed chin and a strangely deformed nose moved towards him, his eyes bright with conspiracy. 'How can we use him?'

'He can buy our freedom.' Morgan had purposefully slowed down, allowing a space to open up between him and Stefan. 'Look at us,' he went on. 'We're not fighters any more, stuck up here in this God-forsaken place. We're doing nothing, going nowhere.'

'So?'

'You want to go back to your family?' Morgan seized hold of the pock-marked man. 'You want to go home? Well, maybe we could. Maybe this William Tell could buy us a pardon.'

'How?' the man with the deformed nose asked.

'Don't you ever listen to nothing, Barber?' Morgan rasped. 'It's this apple business. It's created a stir. The way I hear it is, Gessler wants him – more than he wants any of us. So he'll pay for him, won't he. He'll pay all of us.'

'What about Stefan?' the first bandit – his name was Falcon – asked.

'We don't need him any more,' Morgan whispered. 'Maybe we can include him in the price.'

A slow smile spread over Barber's face and the other man grinned too, revealing a set of teeth as black and as jagged as the mountains themselves. Ahead of them, Stefan and William Tell passed through the broken arches of the castle's entrance. If Morgan had his way, neither man would ever leave.

They feasted that night. Stefan's men had built a huge bonfire out in the open and they had broached a barrel of wine, stolen from a merchant a week before. The food had been prepared by a young woman, barely out of her teens. The last time Tell had seen her she had been no more than a baby. Her mother had died in childbirth. Stefan was her father. Her name was Eleanor.

'This is no life for her,' Stefan growled as he

held out his bowl for a second helping of stew and potatoes. 'I've tried to persuade her to leave . . .'

'And failed.' Eleanor smiled, and not for the first time Tell wondered how so huge and rough a man could have produced so beautiful a daughter. 'I'm happy here with you, Father. There's nowhere else to go.'

'Takes after her mother,' Stefan muttered, and smiled. 'How long can you stay with us, William?' he asked.

'I don't know,' Tell said. 'I have to move . . .'

'Stay with us one day at least. There's something I want to show you. Something you may enjoy.'

None of them got much sleep that night. The feast went on into the small hours. The fire burned low only to be built up again. A second barrel of wine was opened. As the men crouched round the flames, huddling together for warmth, Stefan told the stories that they all knew already but which they were happy to hear again. How Tell had saved Stefan and Stefan had saved Tell. How together they had stolen the Emperor's crown and used the jewels to buy food and weapons for the army that might one day defeat him. In the past they found hope. The future they carefully ignored.

At last they slept, all but Morgan and his two friends. Morgan had said little during the feast, his mind concentrating on the possibilities, planning ahead.

'Barber, Falcon . . .' The bandits drew closer, the flames of the dying fire weaving dark patterns on their faces. 'You must go to Gessler. Get a written pardon from him. Then bring him here.'

'How can you be sure you can trust him?' Falcon asked, scratching at his chin.

'Make sure he only gives you six soldiers,' Morgan replied. 'No more. That way, if they try anything, we'll outnumber them.'

The two bandits nodded in approval.

'As for the pardon . . .' Morgan thought for a moment. 'It's got to be in writing.'

'But we can't read,' Barber reminded him.

'He doesn't know that. But make sure it's sealed with his ring. If it's got his mark on it, that'll be enough.'

The two bandits glanced at Morgan in silent approval. Then they slipped away, disappearing into the shadows of the night.

The next morning, Stefan and Eleanor took Tell round to the other side of the castle compound to show him what they had found.

'We trap wild horses down in the plains and bring them up here to break them,' Stefan explained. 'We brought this one up four days ago.'

As he spoke, he pointed and Tell found himself gazing at the most beautiful animal he had ever seen. It was a pure, dazzling white, at least eighteen hands, with a wild, knotted mane. The horse was built for speed – the horse was speed. It was standing in a wide corral, penned in by the wooden barriers, but Tell knew instinctively that given its freedom it would be away and over the mountains like a crossbow bolt.

'It's beautiful,' he said.

'It's unbreakable,' Stefan added. 'I've never seen a horse like it. A stallion, but with spirit . . .' He turned to Tell. 'Do you want it?'

Tell could only nod in silent awe.

'If you can break it in, you can have it. A present for old times.'

Tell hesitated for a moment. Then he walked forward, unhooking a rope from one corner of the corral, and climbed in. The horse reared away.

'He'll never do it,' Eleanor said.

'He might,' Stefan muttered. 'Those two . . . they're two of a kind.'

But it looked as if Eleanor was right. For three hours, Tell fought with the horse, a contest not of intelligence or strength but of sheer will. He managed to lasso it with the rope, dragged it to within a few feet of himself, but every time he approached it the stallion reared up, forcing him back. Once, he mounted it and sat triumphantly on its back for all of one second. Then he was measuring his length in the dust, his body bruised, his hands rope-burnt.

At last he gave up, returning to Stefan with a mournful shake of his head. 'You're right,' he said. 'It's unbreakable.'

Stefan laughed. 'Too much for you, William?'

'Too much for anyone.'

'I've never seen anything . . .' Eleanor began, then broke off, looking past Tell.

Tell turned round. Morgan had been watching the contest, laughing louder than anyone each time Tell took a tumble. But he wasn't laughing now. He had armed his crossbow. And he was aiming at the stallion.

'What are you doing?' Stefan demanded.

'It's wild,' Morgan replied. 'It's useless to us.'

'But that's no reason . . .' Stefan began.

'No. He's right.'

Tell moved forward and held out a hand for the crossbow. Puzzled, Morgan gave it to him. The stallion had backed away to the far end of the corral as if sensing its danger. Tell aimed with the crossbow and fired. The bolt streaked past the stallion and severed the rope that kept the gate closed. The gate swung open. With one powerful leap, the stallion was free. As Stefan and Eleanor watched, it galloped out of the castle compound and over the first mountain ridge, disappearing into the valley on the other side. Tell handed the crossbow back to a sullen Morgan.

'It's wild,' he said simply. 'It should be free.'

Gessler examined the two men in front of him without trying to conceal his distaste. They had arrived early that morning and the captain of the guard would normally have refused them entry to the castle but for two words that they had stammered out at the gate: William Tell. They knew where he was. They knew how Gessler could find him.

Now they stood in front of him, waiting for him to speak. The one called Falcon seemed to be in charge. The other – with a nose that looked as if it was about to give birth to some monstrous insect – had barely said a word. They smelt, however, equal.

'You say there's a price on your head?' Gessler asked.

'Yes, my lord,' Falcon whispered.

'Well, can you give me one good reason why I shouldn't have it removed from your shoulders?' Gessler smiled. 'I refer, of course, to your head, not to the price.'

Falcon swallowed nervously. 'We have William Tell, my lord,' he said. 'I can lead you to him.'

'Tell?'

'He's in the mountains. I'm to take six soldiers back. No more. And a signed pardon. From you.'

Gessler nodded, his face blank. 'I see. And you say you've been fighting with this man . . . Stefan?'

'Yes, my lord.' Falcon had been chewing his thumb nail. Now, reaching the end, he began to chew his thumb. 'But you can have him too.'

Gessler paused, as if considering the offer. Still

his face gave nothing away. 'Very well,' he said at last. 'Go to the kitchen and get something to eat. I'll send for you later.'

Bowing, the two bandits backed out of the room. Gessler turned to the man who had stood beside him throughout the meeting. It had been annoying losing Tyrrol. Gessler had felt no sadness about the death of his former commander of the guard. If he wasn't good enough to defend himself, he didn't deserve to live. Still, it had been troublesome finding a successor for him, someone who could combine his unique qualities of utter loyalty and ferocious cruelty. But this new man, Horst, was shaping up well. He had killed fifteen peasants already and he had only had the job a few days. Gessler had heard it said that one of the peasants actually died of fright, simply looking into his eyes. He could believe it. Horst had eyes like no others Gessler had seen: black, pitiless, the devil's eyes. The other soldiers were whispering that Horst's mother had been a wolf, but Gessler knew this was not the case. He had met Horst's mother shortly after Horst had arrested her.

'We'll play along with this . . . Falcon,' Gessler muttered, plucking a bunch of grapes out of his fruit bowl. 'At least, that's what we'll let him think. You'll go with him, taking five men with you.' He rolled a grape between thumb and finger. 'But there'll be another ten soldiers riding behind you. It shouldn't be difficult following your trail. Once you get to this mountain hide-out, you know what to do.'

Horst smiled.

'I think I'll go with them,' Gessler went on. 'I've had enough trouble from this William Tell and it will give me great personal satisfaction to deal with him myself. Do you understand?' Gessler squeezed the grape until it exploded, red juice dripping over his fingers. 'Kill Tell. Kill all of them. None of them are to escape alive.'

Stefan was worried. Two days had passed since Tell's arrival at the camp and he was beginning to wish that he hadn't persuaded him to stay and rest before continuing his journey. Only that morning he had noticed that two of the men – Falcon and Barber – were missing. They were Morgan's men through and through. Which meant that Morgan was up to something. Stefan intended to find out what.

Morgan was on look-out when Stefan found him, perched high up in one of the towers. From here you could see ten miles in every direction. But if riders approached, would Morgan raise the alarm? Or was he waiting for them?

'Morgan?' Stefan asked. The bandit turned round to face him. 'I thought Falcon was meant to be on look-out. Not you.'

Morgan shrugged and tried to smile. But the scowl was fixed to his face as if glued there. 'He wasn't around,' he said, 'so I took his place.'

'Where is he?'

'How am I meant to know?'

'He's taken a horse.' Stefan's hand had unconsciously fallen to the knife he wore in his belt. 'You're planning something, aren't you, Morgan? I know you . . .'

There was the crunch of a boot on gravel behind him. Stefan looked back. Two bandits had followed him up the tower. Both carried crossbows. The crossbows were armed. And they were pointing at him.

Morgan shrugged. 'It seems you don't know me quite well enough.'

Ten minutes later, Stefan found himself securely tied, hand and foot. He was sitting in one of the stronger huts, a guard at the door, and he was feeling sick at heart. What made him feel even worse was the fact that he was not alone. William Tell, similarly tied, sat hunched up next to him. They had taken him as he slept. Four of them had come for him and he had never had a chance. There was no sign of Eleanor but Morgan was looking for her too. It could only be a matter of time before she was found.

'You shouldn't have come,' Stefan said.

'I brought trouble,' Tell replied.

'No. The trouble was waiting for you to arrive.' Stefan struggled briefly and gave up. The cords were too tight. At least Morgan had learnt something in the years he had been with him. 'I should have known Morgan would try something . . .'

Tell shrugged as best he could. 'He's a fool if he thinks he can do a deal with Gessler.'

Stefan glanced at the door. The bandit guard was standing a few yards away with his back to them. Even if they managed to get free they had no weapons and he would raise the alarm before they got anywhere near him. Meanwhile, Morgan was waiting for Falcon and Barber. From what he had said, it was clear that they would arrive at any time now.

'Do you think . . . ?' Stefan began.

'Sssh!' Tell's eyes darted upwards. Stefan followed them and frowned. The roof of the hut was made of straw and wattle and as he watched, a blade appeared, sawing through in a circle. Someone was on the roof, cutting a way in. A hand forced its way through, widening the gap, Stefan smiled. Morgan had not yet found Eleanor. But she had found them.

Horst had killed Falcon and Barber as soon as the hide-out had come into sight. He didn't need them any more and two quick deaths now would serve as a pleasant hors d'oeuvre before the banquet to come. According to the two bandits, there were sixteen men and a girl in Stefan's camp. Sitting ducks.

Gessler rode up and joined him with his squadron of black knights. Just as he had suspected, he had had no trouble in following the trail, especially as Horst had helped him by dropping a coloured pebble at every turning. Now they had surprise on their side. They out-numbered their enemy. And Tell was supposedly a prisoner, tied up and helpless. Gessler glanced up at the cloudless sky. It really was going to be a beautiful day.

He gave the signal and they charged.

Morgan knew at once that he had been betrayed. Whatever he might have become, he had once been a good fighter and he quickly rallied his men, refusing to panic. They still had the strength of their position. The black knights would have to ride uphill to attack them and the castle walls would provide them with defence. He lifted his own crossbow and fired. The bolt missed Gessler by inches and thudded into a tree.

For Morgan had miscalculated the speed at which the black knights were riding. They had reached the ruined castle before he knew it and then they were all around him, slashing in all directions. At these close quarters, the bandits were finished before the fight had even begun. Some had been asleep, waking up only to die. Morgan himself managed to take two knights with him, shooting one and strangling another before Horst's sword found him. His head was still scowling when it hit the ground.

Tell, Stefan and Eleanor ran out of the hut and into the middle of this nightmare.

'I've got a horse,' Eleanor shouted. 'At the back . . .'

'Where?' Tell demanded.

'Over there.' Eleanor pointed away from the slaughter. 'But there's only one. Father, I . . .'

'Take it,' Tell interrupted. 'Take it and ride.'

'But you . . .' Stefan began.

'Just do as I say.' Without another word, Tell scooped up a sword and ran forward.

Stefan grabbed hold of Eleanor and began to run. He would have stayed and fought with his friend, but he knew that Tell was right. To have done so would have meant the death of all three of them. Eleanor had tethered the horse to one side of the compound, away from the fighting. Quickly, he hoisted her onto the saddle, then got on behind her. The two of them were away before the black knights even noticed them.

Tell was less fortunate.

He had climbed up onto the battlements and was making for the far tower hoping to find a way down when Gessler stopped him. Gessler had been searching for him from the start, blind to anything else. And now they faced each other on the narrow ledge. Gessler smiled triumphantly. He had learnt sword-fighting in the court of the Emperor himself. He had had the best instructor in the country: Gessler had killed him in their final lesson. He would take Tell single-handed. And he would do it now.

Their swords crossed. Even in the first exchange Tell realized he was hopelessly outmatched. Given a crossbow he would have put Gessler down in a second, no matter what the distance. But the sword was not his weapon. The Governor was raining down blows on him, weaving and slicing with the cold control of a madman. As Tell ducked, he felt a searing pain across his shoulder. Blood welled out of his shirt. He grit his teeth and parried upwards. Another few inches to the left and it would have been his throat.

He struck out again and this time he was lucky, slipping past Gessler's guard and almost finishing it then and there. But Gessler recovered quickly, leaping back with the grace of a dancer, his face flushed with self-confidence. But the move had given Tell a few seconds' thinking time. He glanced downwards. It was a drop of perhaps ten feet to the grass outside the castle. He hurled his sword at Gessler, spinning it like a dagger. Gessler stepped to one side. At the same moment, Tell jumped.

He hit the grass with both feet, rolling over to lessen the impact. He was lucky. If the ground had been less even, he could have broken an ankle. But a few seconds later he was up again and running, putting as much space between himself and the ruined castle as he could.

From his vantage point at the top of the ridge, Stefan watched Tell go. He and Eleanor were safe now. Even if the black knights saw them, they would be able to lose themselves in the twisting mountain paths before anybody could reach them. But it seemed that Tell was lost. He was running down a gentle slope. There was a thick clump of trees about half a mile away. If he could reach it, he might just be able to hide and wait for nightfall. But already Gessler was screaming orders. And the man with the black eyes, along with six riders, were racing after him.

Seven galloping knights against a man on foot. Half a mile to go. Tell didn't have a chance.

Then Stefan saw something gleaming white on the edge of the valley. It had come out of nowhere and it was streaking towards Tell as if to cut him off from the other end. Tell had seen it too. The knights were closer now and gaining ground all the time but even so he had slowed down, stumbling to a complete halt. Stefan felt a thrill of disbelief. It was the stallion. It had come for him, riding out of the sun, drawn as if by some instinct or natural magic to the man who had saved its life.

'Two of a kind, by God!' Stefan muttered. 'Two of a kind.'

The horse had refused to let Tell ride it back in the corral. Out in the open, now that it was free, it bowed its head and waited as Tell sprang up onto its back. The knights were very close now. One of them fired off a shot. But already Tell was away, riding the stallion bareback, and it was flying over the grass towards the forest, its hooves barely touching the ground.

And then they were gone.

Gessler climbed down from the battlements

and walked past the dead or dying bandits, his face dark with anger.

Stefan tugged at his own horse and he and Eleanor rode over the ridge and down into the safety of the mountain pass.

Five: The Mercenary

Gessler was in a bad mood. Everything seemed to have gone wrong for him from the day he had met William Tell. Firstly, the outlaw had escaped from him, not once but twice. The two of them had been face to face at Stefan's mountain hide-out and Gessler had let him get the better of him. It was unthinkable. Worse, it was unspeakable – for what would the Emperor say if he ever found out?

And there were more serious problems for the Emperor to hear of. Gessler's reign of destruction had had an unfortunate side-effect. He had stolen so many farms, burnt so many villages, killed so many people that the whole province was now facing a crisis. Put simply, there just weren't enough peasants left to pay the taxes. The last thing Gessler could risk was a shortfall in his revenues to the central court, so he had been forced to make up the difference out of his own fortunes. This was a disastrous state of affairs. If it went on much longer he would end up like the country. Ruined.

The answer seemed to lie with William Tell. Kill Tell and his run of bad luck might be over. Even if it wasn't, his death would still be something to celebrate.

That was why he was particularly interested in the man that Horst had found.

'You're sure he can rid me of Tell?' Gessler demanded as the two men walked down into the castle courtyard.

'He says he can, my lord,' Horst replied.

'But he's a mercenary!'

'He has quite a reputation, my lord.'

'We'll see.'

Gessler stopped at the entrance to the courtyard and stared disdainfully at the man who stood before him . . . if man was the right word. He was a giant, at least seven foot tall, with hair down to his shoulder blades and a face that must have given his own mother nightmares. He was dressed in leather, his chest bare. He carried only one weapon, a long black rod, circular in shape, with not a blade or bolt in sight.

'My name is De Flores,' the mercenary said. His accent made his words almost incomprehensible but Gessler was moderately surprised that he could talk at all.

'De Flores?' he repeated. 'Yes. I think I've heard that name somewhere before. A mercenary? Tell me, De Flores, what's your price?'

'To kill Tell?' De Flores shrugged. 'Two hundred silver pieces.'

Gessler was flabbergasted and showed it. 'Two hundred? For one man? That's outrageous!'

De Flores shrugged again. With muscles like his, one shrug could have killed an ox. 'If you want the best, you pay for it,' he said simply.

'I've seen better in a freak show,' Gessler sniffed. 'You're wasting my time, De Flores.' He turned to Horst. 'Get rid of him.'

What happened next was very fast. Horst nodded and three black knights walked forward towards the mercenary. They were about six paces away when he moved. Gripping his black rod in one hand, he brought it swinging down. Gessler heard it whistle through the air and then crack as it came into contact with one of the knight's necks. The other two knights had taken out their swords at the first sign of trouble, but they were too slow. De Flores pressed a hidden button on the rod and four blades sprang out of one end. A second knight fell as he swung it forward. The third knight slashed down with his sword, but De Flores had one more trick up his sleeve. He pulled and the black rod broke into two sections, each with a lethal spike at the end. The knight stared at it, then at him, then turned and ran for his life. The life of a palace guard might pay well, with three good meals a day – but 'life' was what it was all about. When Gessler looked again, the fight was over. Two dead, one deserted. And it had only taken five seconds.

'Very impressive,' Gessler muttered. He glanced at the bodies with a sigh of vexation. 'But they were only going to show you the door . . .'

*

William Tell had often had nightmares about his home village while he was in prison, but the reality was even more dreadful. Not a single building had been left standing. Clairmont was a burnt hole in the tapestry of the countryside and even after so many months the smell of death still clung to it. Tell rode by his forge . . . where his forge had been. Now only a few broken beams of wood and a pile of rubble remained. He looked round, hearing the echoes of children laughing, of music and singing in the hollow rustle of the wind. Only the maypole was still standing – whether by a twist of fate or because of some cruel directive of Gessler he could not say. And the hat was on the top, tattered and discoloured by the rain but still recognizable. With a silent groan, Tell plucked it off and threw it down to the ground. There was nothing here for him. If Katrina had been here when the black knights rode in, then she was dead. He spurred on his stallion and rode out again.

He rode for another mile before he came upon an undamaged building. It was a tavern, originally built to service the wealthy merchants and noblemen who passed through on their way to the markets. But nobody came this way any more. The tavern was shabby and had it not been for the single figure of a man, sitting outside it, Tell could have thought it derelict and ridden on. He recognized the man. Dismounting, he walked over and joined him.

Time had joined with the black knights in its cruelty to Brother Gregory. The old priest was almost blind, his face haggard, his hair in disarray. He was drinking clumsily from a wooden cup and even before Tell reached him he could see – and smell – the truth. Brother Gregory was a broken man.

Tell stood over him and the old priest gazed up at him through eyes thick with cataracts and tears. 'William . . . ?' he muttered. His lips were trembling.

'Where is she, Gregory?' Tell asked. 'Katrina . . .'

The priest drank from the cup but said nothing.

'You were her friend, Gregory,' Tell went on. 'She must have told you. Unless . . .'

'No. She's not dead. But . . .' The priest waved a hand towards the door. 'Sit down, William. Have something to drink.'

A young girl came out of the tavern carrying a pitcher and another cup. Tell sat down and sniffed the liquid that was being poured for him. It was golden in colour and smelt of prunes. It was some sort of wine, but stronger than anything he had ever tasted before.

'It's burnt wine,* William,' Gregory explained. 'The best. Fiery stuff in more ways than one. They've managed to make a living for themselves

* Burnt wine – from the German word, *branntwein*. Nowadays we'd call it brandy, though smelling of prunes this must be some sort of armagnac.

here at the tavern. The young girl is my niece. Her mother is my sister. They're looking after me now.' Brother Gregory raised his cup. 'I never thought I'd see you again.'

'Where is she, Gregory?'

The old man drank heavily as if afraid of what he had to say. When at last he spoke, his voice was low. 'I can't tell you. After . . . what happened, she left. There was nothing for her here. And they said . . . they said you killed Matthew. I never believed it. I told her it wasn't true. But then they brought a body . . .' Brother Gregory paused. 'What did happen, William?'

'Just tell me where she went.'

'I can't. She made me swear. I swore on the Bible, William, and I have to keep that oath. I'm a priest, remember. I was a priest . . .'

Tell got up and walked into the tavern. He remembered the time when it had been a hive of activity, filled with laughing, drinking people, the sort of place he had warned Matthew against. Now it was empty. An old woman was filling another jug from two huge barrels that stood against the wall. The girl was sweeping. There was nobody else in there.

'You can stay the night here if you want,' the old woman said.

Tell shook his head. 'No. It's not safe . . . not for you or your daughter.'

'We can hide you.'

'No. I'll sleep out tonight. And tomorrow I'll

leave.' Tell turned round and walked out again. As he went, he muttered something else, but the old woman didn't hear him: 'I have no place here any more.'

The mercenary reached the tavern later that night. He was no longer alone. Four men rode with him, each as repulsive as he was, in their own ways. One was horrendously fat. One was quite bald, with a nose so broken as to be almost hanging off his face. One had no teeth. The last was missing an ear. They were dressed, like De Flores, in leather straps. Unlike him, they were bristling with weapons: crossbows, swords, daggers, axes, maces, mangles and chains.

'Bosola!' As De Flores called out, the bald mercenary rode forward to join him. 'Tell me about this man, William Tell,' De Flores demanded.

'Don't you know?' Bosola spat. 'He was the one who shot the apple off the boy's head.'

'Ah yes . . .' De Flores smiled unpleasantly. 'But I heard he missed and killed the boy.'

'That's what some people say. Nobody knows for sure.'

De Flores considered for a moment. 'An apple?' he muttered. 'Quite a shot. Perhaps he can give us a demonstration.'

'If we find him.'

'We'll find him.' De Flores laughed. 'We'll find him all right.'

Their arrival at the tavern was no coincidence.

William Tell had so far been sighted twice since his escape from Death Castle – first at Isabel's farm, then at Stefan's hide-out. He was heading south and it hadn't taken much guesswork on Gessler's part to realize where he was heading. He had to go back to Clairmont, to find out what had happened to his wife. It was only a three-day ride from the mountains, so he would turn up there any time now. And De Flores would be waiting for him.

But as the mercenaries reined in their horses and dismounted outside the tavern, De Flores saw that he wouldn't have to wait after all. Gessler had described the white stallion that had come to his rescue and there it was, tethered outside. So William Tell was nearby, perhaps even inside.

De Flores was looking forward very much to meeting him.

William Tell opened his eyes, aware that something was wrong even before he fully regained consciousness. He had been sleeping out in the open, not far from the tavern. What had woken him up? There was no sound. Nobody was near him. But something inside him was screaming at him. Wake up. Get away. There's danger . . .

He pushed the blanket off him and rolled onto one knee, reaching at the same time for his crossbow. An owl or some nightbird fluttered in a tree above him and for one moment his eyes flickered upwards. It was a warm night. A full moon shone, throwing crystal shadows through the silent forest. Edging forward, he thrust a hand out and pressed the undergrowth down so that he could look out towards the tavern.

'Tell!'

The voice was hard, pitiless, echoing through the night. Two torches burnt outside the tavern, fixed on each side of the door. A man stood there, a black silhouette against the open doorway, his shadow stretching out towards the forest. He was huge. That was the first thing that Tell registered. Then he saw the other four men. They had stretched out across the open ground in front of the tavern. They were armed. And they had taken prisoners. The old woman and the young girl had been dragged out of bed and stood shivering in their nightclothes. Brother Gregory was kneeling on the ground. Tell could just make out a trickle of blood, running down the side of his face. The big man was holding some sort of rod, its end pointing at the priest's neck.

'I know you're there, Tell!' De Flores called out. 'We have hostages. The old man will die if you don't come out. And he'll only be the first.'

Tell hesitated. From where he was hiding, he could take out the mercenary leader with one well-aimed bolt. But that would mean certain death for the two women. He could turn and run. The result would be the same and without his horse he would be easily hunted down. Whoever this man was – a mercenary of some sort – he held all the cards. Tell came to a decision. Throwing down his crossbar he stood up and walked into the light.

'I never thought it would be so easy,' Bosola said, moving forward to cover him.

De Flores laughed. 'I knew he'd come.'

'How?'

'Because he's a hero!'

Tell had not spoken a word. Bosola eyed him like a butcher examining a slab of meat. He was carrying an axe and suddenly he struck out, the handle driving into Tell's neck. Tell fell soundlessly. Bosola spat.

'So he shot an apple . . .' De Flores muttered to himself.

'What of it?' Bosola had taken a length of rope from his belt and was about to tie Tell's hands.

'Don't tie him.' De Flores glanced at the young girl, cowering beside her mother. 'Tie the girl.'

'Why?'

'We're going to do it again. The apple.'

Tell woke up slowly, a pain throbbing in the side of his head. He was lying where he had fallen. How long had he been there? The first thing he heard was laughter. The mercenaries had found the burnt wine and had helped themselves. From the sound of them, they were halfway drunk, but Tell knew that didn't make them any less dangerous. He moved his hands and realized that he hadn't been tied. That meant they had something else in mind. He opened his eyes.

The girl was sitting on a stool in front of the tavern, her hands behind her back. Three of the mercenaries were stretched out on the ground, drinking from wooden cups. The fourth held a crossbow, aimed at Tell. There was no sign of Brother Gregory.

De Flores strolled forward and stood over him. 'Ah, so you're with us again, Tell,' he mocked. 'That's good. You see, there's something you can do for me. I want to see this for myself. The legend.' De Flores held a cup in his hand. He drained it, the burnt wine spilling out of the corner of his mouth. 'But this time I'm going to make it easier for you. Not an apple. A goblet.' He turned round and balanced the goblet on the terrified girl's head. 'If you speak one word or move one inch, I'll cut your throat,' he warned her.

Tell got to his feet.

'You miss and I kill her myself. Then we do it again with the priest. You understand?' De Flores was enjoying himself. The two hundred silver pieces were as good as his, but Tell had disappointed him. He had been expecting more of a challenge. Well, he would have his fun all right. This was only the start. 'Give him a crossbow!' he called out.

One of the mercenaries moved towards him but De Flores stopped him. 'No. You keep him covered. Old man!' Brother Gregory appeared from inside the tavern. 'You do it, old man,' De Flores commanded. 'After all, you're the next target if he misses.'

The mercenaries bellowed with laughter as Gregory picked up a crossbow and carried it over to Tell. Quickly Tell looked around him. The leader knew what he was doing. He was making sure his men kept their distance, allowing him no chance to get near them. Quickly, he took stock of his surroundings. The wood behind him. The girl on the stool. A torch burning on each side of the door. The shadowy interior of the tavern. The gentle slope of the ground. Suddenly he knew what he had to do. Everything depended on De Flores. How long would he want to prolong the game?

Tell took the crossbow. 'Gregory,' he whispered. 'Untie my horse. Do you understand?'

Gregory nodded.

'Hold onto it and wait . . .'

Tell loaded the crossbow as Gregory shuffled away into the darkness, momentarily forgotten. All eyes were on Tell now. The five mercenaries had got to their feet and formed a group to the left of the door, some distance away from the girl. The mother had been left where she was, huddled on the ground on the other side, not daring even to look. Tell resisted the temptation to smile. It couldn't have been better if he had planned it himself.

He swept the crossbow up to his shoulder,

aimed and fired. De Flores's smile vanished. The bolt had passed harmlessly over the girl's head, disappearing into the tavern. It hadn't even gone close. At the same time, she had jerked to one side, knocking over the cup.

'You missed on purpose!' De Flores screamed. 'You didn't even try!' He pressed the button on his black rod and the knife blades sprang out again. 'Do you want me to kill her?' he demanded.

'No!' Tell lowered the crossbow. 'Wait!'

'Wait? What for?'

'Give me a second chance.' Tell allowed a pitiful whine to enter his voice. 'Please . . .'

'Why should I?'

'Because you don't believe I can do it. Let me show you. I can!'

De Flores was enjoying his sense of power. He laughed scornfully. 'You're right,' he said. 'I don't believe you can do it. I don't believe you ever did. Two hundred silver pieces for you? I wouldn't have paid twenty . . .'

'Please . . .' Tell was almost on his knees.

De Flores considered, then reached out. Bosola gave him a second bolt and he threw it at Tell. 'All right,' he said. 'I'll give you another chance. Only this time I'll make it more difficult for you. Not a goblet . . .' He went over to the girl and placed something on her head. 'A silver piece. And this time you'd better not miss.'

Although De Flores didn't know it, Tell hadn't

missed with his first bolt either. It had found its target inside the tavern, the tap on one of the two barrels. With perfect accuracy it had knocked the top clean off and even as De Flores had talked, burnt wine had been pouring out onto the floor. The tavern was built on a slight slope. The burnt wine had formed a miniature river running out and then turning to form a pool around the mercenary's feet. They were standing in the middle of it now, but with their eyes fixed on Tell, none of them had seen it.

Tell reloaded and raised the crossbow for a second time. The silver piece was almost invisible, lost in the girl's hair, but that didn't concern him. His target was above her, burning beside the door. He fired and the bolt knocked one of the torches out of its holder. De Flores just had time to register that once again Tell had cheated him when the whole world exploded around him.

The torch had hit the burnt wine. The burnt wine had ignited.

Screaming, the mercenaries found themselves trapped in a prison of fire. They had spilt the burnt wine on their clothes as they drank and now the flames found it, racing up their bodies, devouring them where they stood. It was a horrible sight, but Tell had no time to watch. Already he was running. Brother Gregory had released his horse. The white stallion was speeding towards him.

As the girl ran away from the nightmare, Tell

mounted the horse. He paused just long enough to check that the girl had got away – and her mother with her – then he reined forward. The stallion leapt over the flames and galloped away into the night.

But De Flores wasn't finished. His boots and trousers were alight, the flames all around him, but the thick leather was protecting his flesh. As the fire had leapt up, he had grabbed a crossbow from Bosola. Now, ignoring the screams of his men and the fact that he was himself beginning to burn, he fired.

The bolt hit Tell high up in the shoulder as he rode out.

Tell staggered, almost thrown out of his saddle by the force of the impact. Had he been any closer when De Flores fired, the shock would have killed him. But somehow he managed to stay upright. With a numbness spreading through his back and neck he rode on into the night. Soon he could feel nothing at all. His hand was sticky and, lifting it, he saw that it was covered in his own blood. Still he rode on. The mercenary was alive. He would come after him. It wasn't over yet.

As dawn broke and the first streaks of pink and orange appeared in the sky, Tell slid out of his saddle and crashed to the ground. He was still lying there when the sun rose and the new day began.

Six: The Convent

'He can't have gone far. We'll find him.'

De Flores was kneeling over a stream, washing his face. He had changed since the night before. Gone was the arrogant self-confidence and sense of power. Gone also was most of his hair. The flames had not left him looking a pretty sight and he had been no beauty to begin with. He could hardly believe it. He had had William Tell in the palm of his hand and through his own vanity he had let him get away. De Flores had never failed, not once in his life. His reputation depended on it. But now he had been knocked off his perch. One of his mercenaries was dead. Another – Antonio – probably wouldn't survive the day. That left just two men. Flamineo, the man without the ear, had escaped the worst of the flames. Bosola had saved himself by diving head-first into a well.

'We should have gone after him last night.' Bosola scowled. 'While we still had him.'

'While *we* had *him*?' De Flores almost screamed. 'There were five of us yesterday. Now look at us! Three and a half!'

Bosola looked down at the silent figure of

Antonio. Suddenly he felt old and tired. 'He can't ride much further with those burns,' he said.

'Then get rid of him!' De Flores snapped. 'He'll only hold us up.'

Bosola swallowed. It hurt him to swallow – but then it hurt him to do just about anything. He glanced at Antonio. The two men had ridden together for ten years. If Bosola could say that he had a single friend in the world, it was probably Antonio. 'Tell can't have gone far,' he said. 'He was wounded. He's probably dead already.'

'I hope not, Bosola.' De Flores reached for his horse. 'I hope not. I have a score to settle with William Tell. I want to find him alive.'

'And then?'

'And then I'll pay him back . . .' De Flores pulled his stirrups tight, ready to leave. 'Come on,' he said. 'Let's move.'

'We can't move!' Bosola jerked a thumb in the direction of Antonio. 'He can't move. He's burnt. Haven't you looked at him? He was in the middle of it. He can't ride any more. He needs help.'

De Flores paused for a moment, resting against his horse. When he pulled away, he was holding his black rod. He wrenched it apart, the two knife blades curving inwards. Then, without another word, he slammed both pieces downwards. Antonio groaned and lay still. Bosola stared, his mouth open. De Flores straightened up, wiping the blades on his trousers. 'Well,' he muttered, 'you said he needed help.'

He joined the rod together again and mounted his horse.

'Let's get started!' he said. 'I want to find Tell.'

William Tell was lying on a narrow bed in a clean, whitewashed room. The room was in some sort of monastery. He could tell from the sound of the bell that was chiming outside and from the crucifix that hung on the wall above him. He had no idea how he had got there or how long he had been there. The light, streaming in through the room's single window, suggested an afternoon sun. Someone had taken the bolt out of his shoulder and dressed the wound, using a tourniquet to staunch the bleeding. His whole arm was supported by a sling, tied behind his neck. He tested himself, clenching and unclenching his fingers. It hurt him, but everything seemed to be working properly.

The door opened and a figure walked in. So it wasn't a monastery but a convent. The nun had bowed her head. He couldn't see her face. Gently, she closed the door behind her and came into the room. Only when she had sat on the bed did she look up. Tell gasped. It was Katrina.

For a long while neither of them spoke. Then Tell pulled her towards him and kissed her on the lips. In that brief moment he knew that he had found her and lost her at the same time. She came to him unwillingly, pulling away. Was it just the clothes she was wearing, the nun's habit, that separated her from him? Was she forbidden perhaps to have any physical contact with him? But wherever she was, whatever she had become, she was still Tell's wife. What separated them was something deeper, something more final.

'I thought you were dead,' she said at last.

'Why, Katrina?' Tell could only stare at her. 'Why this?'

'What else was there for me to do?' Tears had sprung to her eyes. 'I was alone. The village was in ruins. You were gone. I had no one else to turn to.'

'But . . . a nun?'

'I'm a novice, not a nun. They've given me shelter. Later on, perhaps, I'll join the order.'

'But why?' Suddenly Tell was angry. He had travelled a long way in search of his wife. And now that he had found her she wanted only to reject him.

'You never understood me, did you?' Katrina wiped a hand across her eyes. 'I always knew that one day it would come back . . . the fighting, the violence. That's all you ever were . . . a killer. And that day, when they took Matthew . . .'

'That wasn't my fault.'

'He was his father's son. I'd always known it would happen. One way or another . . .'

'Where is Matthew?' Tell asked softly.

'I'll show you.'

She helped him off the bed and together they

walked through the convent. After the rigours of the mountains and the countryside, Tell had to admit that Katrina had at least found a perfect haven, a place of tranquillity and rest. It was a small convent, built on two floors around a central garden with a fountain sparkling under the sun. Other nuns were walking around the cloister, some reading, some deep in meditation. A bell-tower rose up in one corner, the bricks a cheerful fretwork of pink and blue. Beneath the bell-tower, two doors led into the main chapel. Katrina and Tell followed a narrow passage out of the cloister, past the kitchen and laundry area and finally out of the convent altogether. The passage led to a cemetery.

Katrina stood in front of a grave. It was marked with a simple wooden cross. but with no name. Fresh flowers had been scattered at its foot. Tell guessed that every day new flowers would take their place.

'Gessler brought him here to be buried,' Katrina said. She could not keep the hatred out of her voice. 'After you killed him.'

'No!' Tell took her arm. 'That's not how it happened.'

'They say there was some sort of challenge. You fired and hit him. They told me you killed him, William.'

'No! You're wrong.' Katrina was refusing to look into his eyes and now he understood the gulf that had come between them. He swung her round and forced her to meet him eye to eye. 'They're lying, Katrina. That's what they want you to believe. But it didn't happen that way.'

'But . . .' Katrina turned back towards the grave.

'Did you ever see the body? Did Gessler show it to you?'

'No.'

'And will you really believe him before you believe me?'

'I . . .' Katrina couldn't hold back the tears. She couldn't speak.

'There was a challenge, but I never harmed Matthew. He's still alive. I know it. I can feel it. Matthew is alive and I'm going to find him.'

Tell drew Katrina closer to him and this time she didn't resist. Still crying, her head against his chest, she allowed him to embrace her and arm in arm they turned away from the grave and made their way back into the convent.

De Flores was getting closer.

It was an easy trail to follow. Every few yards he came upon a drop of blood pointing the way as clearly as a signpost. Then Bosola found Tell's horse, wandering loose in a field.

'It's his horse all right,' Bosola said. 'And his crossbow's with it.'

'So he's unarmed.' De Flores smiled for the first time that day. 'And he's near.'

'But where?' Bosola gazed across the countryside. There was no sign of anyone. Just then a bell rang out in the distance. De Flores twisted round, his eyes narrowing.

'A monastery?' Bosola asked.

De Flores smiled again and now his whole face was distorted by a surge of pleasure that wasn't quite human. 'Yes,' he said, 'or maybe a convent . . .'

The abbess was very old. She had been brought to the convent as a child and had been there all her life. Now her skin was wrinkled and her eyesight was fading but her mind was as sharp as it had always been. When the man – William Tell – was brought to her, she greeted him with the same stern familiarity that she used with her novices. The fact that he was a soldier, an outlaw, didn't bother her. He needed help. That was all that mattered.

'Sit down,' she commanded, waving him to a chair. Tell sat down with Katrina next to him. 'You shouldn't be out of bed,' the abbess scolded him. 'You're not well enough.'

She put down the book she had been reading, a handwritten copy of Aristotle's *Poetics*, and examined her uninvited guest. 'So you're the famous William Tell, are you?' she said. 'You're very lucky to be alive. If the sisters hadn't found you lying out there in the road, who knows what might have happened?'

'They shouldn't have brought him here,' Katrina said, lowering her eyes.

'Really, Katrina dear!' The abbess sniffed. 'They could hardly have left him, could they? I mean, if we turned up our noses at every wounded man we came across, we'd hardly be nuns, would we!'

'But she's right,' Tell said, unsure quite how to address this indomitable old woman. 'There's at least one man following me. Perhaps more. They can't find me here.'

'He has to leave,' Katrina said.

'I can't leave either,' Tell sighed. 'The men are mercenaries, paid killers. If they discover that I've been here, that you've helped me, there's no saying what they'll do.'

'What is there here for them?' the abbess demanded.

'The gold and silver on the altar. But worse than that . . . these men are unstoppable. They'll kill, simply because that's what they enjoy.'

'What do you suggest we do?'

Tell knew there was only one answer. Wounded and unarmed he was a sitting target and with him out of the way the mercenaries would be free to start on the convent. He dreaded to think what would happen to the nuns in their hands. But would the abbess even consider the alternative?

'I need a weapon,' he said. 'A crossbow. With a crossbow I can surprise them and take out one

. . . maybe two before they can act.' He shook his head. 'There's no other way.'

The abbess had listened to all this in silence but now she raised her arms in a gesture of defeat. Her face was sad. 'My son,' she said, 'you can stay or you can go. That is for you to decide. But you cannot ask for a weapon. This is a house of God.'

'And what do you expect them to do when they get here?' Tell asked. 'Pray?'

'They will do what they must do.' The abbess's voice was final. 'That is all. There are no weapons here.'

Tell marched through the convent with Katrina doing her best to keep up. 'I told you she wouldn't listen,' she was saying. 'So what are you going to do?'

'I need a weapon,' Tell said.

'But there aren't any weapons. Not here . . .'

'We'll see . . .'

He was running out of time and he knew it. The mercenaries would have little trouble following him and they might arrive at the convent at any moment. He passed through the cloisters and back into the room where he had woken up. The tourniquet that the sisters had used to bind his wound still lay beside the bed. He picked it up and tugged at it. As he had suspected, it was made of cat-gut. That was a start.

Then, still followed by Katrina, he went back

out to the graveyard. The little wooden cross that supposedly marked his son's grave stood waiting for him. He plucked it out of the ground. There was nothing holy about the cross, Tell knew. His son wasn't there. It was a trick of Gessler's, nothing more. Well now he would use it his own way.

'What are you doing?' Katrina asked.

'What I have to. Just stay out of my way. Do you understand?'

Katrina nodded. But she didn't understand anything.

In the next five minutes, Tell had scavenged four pieces of string and a handful of nails from the convent. Using the kitchen knife, he had gouged a long groove in the graveyard cross. He had torn a decorative moulding off a pulpit, and he had taken an iron poker out of a fire. It was only then that Katrina realized what was in his mind. It was crude, certainly. But the cross, with the moulding around the end, the groove, the cat-gut and the poker was nonetheless recognizable.

A crossbow.

It was no sooner finished than Tell heard the convent door slam open, the sound itself violent and out-of-place in this house of peace. Tell was in the chapel now, untying a rope that was fixed against the wall. The rope held up a metal chandelier, its circles surmounted by candles. Hearing the sound, he glanced up.

'They're here,' he said. 'Find them. Tell them where I am.'

'No . . .' Katrina couldn't believe what she was being asked to do.

'Do it, Katrina. I've got to take them on my own terms. So they've got to come to me. Just find them and bring them here. Before someone gets killed.'

Katrina left the chapel. Outside in the cloisters, the nuns were running in panic. De Flores had arrived. He was with the abbess. True evil had at last come to the convent.

De Flores was in a good mood. He had gone to church only once in his life and then it was to burn it down. The convent offered all sorts of possibilities, things that no sane mind could have considered.

'So you're the mother, are you, Mother?' he demanded, confronting the old woman across her desk.

'What do you want with us?' the abbess asked. If she was frightened she didn't show it.

'We're looking for a man,' De Flores said. 'We think he's here. And if he is here . . .' He lifted his black rod. Bosola giggled. 'He's wanted, you see,' De Flores went on. 'An outlaw. And if he is here . . . well, that makes you an outlaw too.' Slowly, he moved forward. His thumb found the button on the rod and the blades sprung out. 'Where is he, you horrible old woman?'

'This is a holy place!' Two pin-pricks of red

had appeared in the abbess's cheeks. 'He has sanctuary here.'

'Sanctuary?' De Flores spat. 'He has no sanctuary. None of you have. Do you want to see me tear the place down? Do you want me to show you what happens to traitors?'

'I won't tell you anything!'

'But I will . . .'

Katrina had run all the way to the abbess's chamber and stood in the doorway, out-of-breath. 'He's in the chapel.'

There was a moment's pause. De Flores backed away from the abbess, who looked at Katrina with reproachful eyes. 'He told me to tell them,' Katrina said.

'He did?' De Flores smiled. 'How very good of him.' Followed by the two mercenaries, he walked over to the door. But before he went he turned back to the abbess and stared at her with hatred in his eyes. 'You'll be seeing me again soon,' he promised.

It was dark inside the chapel. The windows were small and Tell had blown out all the candles in the chandelier. The three mercenaries stood in the doorway, waiting while their eyes got used to the light. For a few seconds they couldn't see him. Then Bosola pointed. Tell was sitting in front of the altar with what looked like a wooden cross on his lap. De Flores laughed. 'Cowering behind a cross?' he asked. 'Do you really think that's going to do any good?'

'Wait . . .' Bosola began.

It was the last word he ever spoke. Tell released the cat-gut and the iron poker shot across the chapel, burying itself in his chest. He was dead before he knew what had happened. At the same time, Tell sprang to his feet and ran for a door behind the altar. De Flores stared, rooted to the spot. What he had just seen was impossible. This man was impossible.

'Get after him!' he shouted.

The third mercenary, Flamineo, ran into the shadows of the chapel while De Flores backed out the way he had come in, hoping to catch Tell round the side. But Tell was still inside the chapel, crouching beside the door. As Flamineo crossed the central aisle, Tell lashed out with the knife he had taken from the kitchen. The rope that held the chandelier was just above his head. It was still tied, but while he waited for the mercenaries, Tell had weakened it. One final cut was all it took. The rope broke and the chandelier plummeted down. Flamineo was right underneath it.

Tell heard the man's last despairing shout, but already he was moving, making for the side door. There was a terrible crash behind him but then he was out, moving away from the chapel, down the passage that led through the kitchens. The nuns had been at work on the evening meal when De Flores had arrived. Soup bubbled in a huge cauldron over an open fire. Loaves of bread, fresh out of the oven, lay cooling on the wooden table. Moving quietly now, Tell crept towards the back door. De Flores was loose in the convent. De Flores was the most dangerous of them all.

A shadow saved his life. He saw it on the table a second before De Flores's hand slashed down, the spiked rod missing Tell's head by inches. Ducking to one side, Tell threw himself onto the table. The spike slammed into the wood. For a moment De Flores's face was right beside him and he could feel the man's rank breath on his cheek. His hand stretched out, found a metal stanchion, pulled. The cauldron of soup tipped away from the wall. Tell rolled aside. Three gallons of hot soup poured onto the table. De Flores shrieked. Tell ran for the door and vanished.

But still De Flores came after him. The man was not human. Burnt, soaked and humiliated, only hate sustained him. Half-covered with steaming, slimy vegetables, he staggered out into the open air. He had split his black rod into two sections. All the blades were out. Whimpering with pain and anger, he searched for Tell.

This was the laundry area of the convent. White sheets hung from lines, flapping in the breeze. Slowly, De Flores stalked through them, his knives ready to strike. Tell was here somewhere. He had to be. There was no other way out of the courtyard. Now there were sheets on both sides of him, dazzling in the afternoon sun. The sheets were a maze. He was enclosed, blinded by them. Steam rose from sodden clothes. His eyes, almost lost in his swollen cheeks, darted left and right.

There was a sound behind him. He spun round.

Katrina stood in the doorway of the kitchen. She saw the misshapen creature who had brought death to the convent. He was standing with a weapon in each hand. And he had seen her. He made as if to move towards her but then he froze. His mouth fell open. A red stain spread through the sheet behind him. He groaned, then slumped to his knees, dragging the sheet with him. And with the sheet gone, William Tell stood revealed, the knife still in his hand.

Katrina ran to him.

Tell left that night and he left alone. Katrina had wanted to go with him but he had refused.

'It's too dangerous. You're safe here. You can wait for me. I'll be back. And Matthew will be with me.'

She watched him go with a sadness greater than any she had known. He had promised he would come back. She had no doubt that he would keep his word. But Katrina remembered the look on his face the moment after he had killed De Flores. There had been no pleasure, only a quiet acceptance of what must be.

He was William Tell. A hero, a freedom-fighter

. . . you could call him what you liked. But it seemed to Katrina that the William Tell she had known and loved was gone for ever.

Seven: The Dukes

The three Dukes were very old and very odd. They were seated in thrones lined up in a row on the edge of a castle courtyard. The thrones, like the Dukes, had seen better days. One was missing a leg and had been hastily propped up with bricks. Another had no arms. The third was barely a throne at all but a large crate, covered in mouldy red velvet with a tatter of gold brocade.

The Dukes could have been brothers. But beneath the wrinkles and the straggling hair, the layer of grey dust and the cloaks patched together from various blankets, they could have been anything. All three were well in their eighties and, from the looks of things were unlikely to go too far into their nineties. One, a thin, shrivelled man, had a racking cough. The next, sitting slumped with a toothless smile, had obviously lapsed into idiocy. The last was fat, with rubbery lips and dog-like eyes. He was the healthiest of the three of them and he was unable to walk. He held a sceptre in his left hand. The sceptre was made of wood, decorated with a coil of string.

He raised the sceptre. 'Let the judgement begin.'

They were not alone in the courtyard. Soldiers in rusting armour with rusting swords lined the stairways and battlements. They all looked like the survivors of a particularly nasty battle. The courtyard was strewn with litter. A few mangy dogs lay curled up on the cold stone, licking at their sores.

As soon as the Duke had spoken, a man stepped forward. He was the youngest person present, barely fifty, and also the best dressed. It was true that the moths had made a meal of his cloak and trousers, but at least they fitted and the material had some hint of colour. He was quite bald, with a face like a toad, swollen at the cheeks and slightly green. He stopped underneath a flag that was hanging limply from a splintered pole. With a grand gesture he unfurled a sheet of parchment, cleared his throat and spoke.

'My lords,' he began, 'we are here to settle a dispute of land. The Marquis of Stein and the most noble Duke of Anjuny both lay claim to a valley that stands between their rightful domains. The matter will be dealt with as you have decreed.' He rolled the parchment up again and nodded at a soldier. 'Bring out the plaintiffs.'

The plaintiffs were certainly plain. But two men who looked less like a Marquis or a Duke would have been impossible to imagine. They were peasants, both of them, unshaven, dirty, naked to the waist. As they were led out into the sunlight, they blinked and looked around them.

Both of them looked dazed, as if they had just woken up from a dream . . . or just walked into a nightmare.

They were joined together at the wrist. A thick leather strap about six feet long ran from one to the other. The man with the parchment gestured again and a soldier stepped forward carrying two huge knives; slaughterhouse knives. The blades had been polished and glinted in the sun. The handles were dark brown, encrusted with dried blood.

'A duel to the death, my lords,' the steward cried out, addressing the three old men once again. 'The winner will keep the valley. The loser will be buried in it.' He turned back to the two peasants. 'You have nothing to say?'

The peasants had no idea what he was talking about. They knew only that they had to fight, that refusal would mean death for both of them. They shook their heads mutely.

'Let the duel commence!'

The steward walked to the side of the courtyard and, watched by the Dukes, the two fighters raised their knives and faced each other. The leather band was stretched tight between them. Only six feet separated them, and with the blades curving out of their outstretched hands, that distance seemed even less. It was a vicious form of duel. Space was everything. Step back too far and you would pull your opponent on top of you. Go in too close and you risked impaling yourself on his knife. Each time you moved your knife you would tug on the band and move the other, signalling your own strategy before you had time to put it in effect. Stab forward and you would ease the tension on the band and give the other man a chance to cut you down.

Breathing space. But one false move and you would breathe your last.

The peasants were evenly matched. One was thickset and tall. His movements would be slow, but he had extra strength on his side. The other was a thin whippet of a man. He was balancing on the balls of his feet like a dancer, ready to dodge at the first hint of an attack.

For the first few minutes they sized each other up. It didn't matter now what names they had been given or what roles they were supposed to play. All that mattered was survival. Then the big man stabbed forward. The other – he had been called the Duke of Anjuny – ducked down and the knife passed harmlessly over his shoulder. At the same time, he slashed upwards. The soldiers muttered amongst themselves. They had all placed bets on the outcome. They always placed bets. The Marquis of Stein had drawn blood . . . a flesh wound, nothing more. But the fight had almost been over in the first exchange.

The two men wheeled round each other, the band stretched taut again. Then the heavier man tried another tactic, leaning back and using his strength to draw the other towards him; a deadly tug-of-war. The Marquis of Stein tried to resist, digging his heels into the dust. But inch by inch, a fish on a line, he was pulled in. Now the other man's blade was only a foot away. One more tug and the Duke of Anjuny would have him within arm-reach. Then he would die.

But at the last second, the Marquis of Stein sprang forward. The move took the Duke of Anjuny by surprise. Thrown off balance he tried to recover his footing, but too late. The smaller man's knife swung upwards. With a groan, the Duke of Anjuny sprawled forward, his own knife falling from his lifeless hand.

The duel was over. The Marquis of Stein had won.

'The Marquis of Stein is the victor, my lords,' the steward announced, although this much must have been obvious even to the most idiotic of the lords. 'He will be released and his lands will be returned to him.'

The peasant stood panting in the courtyard. The three old men beamed at him as if they had just done him a favour. Then they chattered amongst themselves.

'Well, let's have dinner, then,' the first said.

'What's for dinner?' the second asked.

'Dinner,' the third replied.

The second Duke was puzzled. 'You mean . . . there's dinner for dinner?'

'Dinner,' the first agreed.

'Ah!' The third Duke understood now. 'Dinner!'

Two of them stood up and helped the third to his feet. His legs hung uselessly beneath him, but somehow they managed to drag him back into the castle. The steward waited until they had gone, then he turned round to look at the victorious peasant, who was standing in the courtyard, still tied to the dead man.

'Kill him.' the steward said.

The peasant just had time to realize that he had been tricked, that he should never have fought the duel in the first place, when the soldiers cut him down.

The storm had come from nowhere. One moment the sky had been clear, the early morning sun pale in the sky. Only the wind, tugging at the tufts of wild grass, has whispered its warning. Then darkness had fallen, smothering up the landscape. The rain had begun, thin at first, rapidly filling out until the very air seemed to have turned into water. The thunder came almost too late. With the rain crashing against the ground, bubbling in puddles that spilled over into rushing, gurgling streams, it could hardly be heard, and the lightning, slicing down across the mountains, seemed to belong to another, distant world.

William Tell pressed forward, leading his horse behind him. He could not ride any more. He could barely walk. The rain was battering against him, slamming against his shoulders as if attempting to force him down into the freezing mud that sucked at him from below. The thunder boomed again, louder than ever, and his horse pulled back nervously, braying in fear. He had to find shelter. Much more of this and they would both be too exhausted to continue.

The lightning crackled and for an instant he saw it, the black silhouette of a castle perched like some huge bird of prey on the edge of a hill. It seemed to be moulded out of the same rock on which it stood, its four towers twisting and sprouting out of the hillside and the whole thing leaning crazily at an angle. But it was shelter. There was somebody living there. In the darkness he could make out the glow of a fire burning red behind two windows that were its eyes.

The castle was about a mile away. Tell knew that any fortified building was potentially dangerous. Once he was inside it he could find himself in a garrison of soldiers, the headquarters of a Governor friendly to Gessler, even an outpost of the Emperor himself. But he had no choice. This was killing weather.

Tightening his grip on the reins he forced himself through the billowing curtain of rain and made for it.

The three Dukes had barely noticed the rain even though it was cascading through a hole in the ceiling and pattering down onto the cold paving stones of the great hall. They were sitting behind a long wooden table surrounded by servants and attendants who, a few hours before, had been soldiers. One of the soldiers was attempting to juggle, his balls and skittles tumbling all around him. Three soldiers, dressed as minstrels, plucked clumsily at harps, the wrong notes so frequent that they completely hid the right ones. Each Duke had been served with a baked potato on a tin plate. And the Dukes were delighted.

'Beef,' said the first.

'Lamb,' exclaimed the second.

'Pheasant,' muttered the third.

The steward who had condemned the two peasants to death stood respectfully to one side, overseeing the banquet. He clicked his finger and another servant ran forward with a buckled pitcher of ordinary spring water. He poured it and the three Dukes tasted it, smacking their lips as if it were the finest vintage wine . . . which, in fact, they thought it was. To anybody watching it would have been perfectly plain that the three men were totally senile, but the steward gazed at them only with respect. His name was Lascal and he had served them for twenty years, ever since he was a boy.

'Where is the messenger, Lascal?' the first Duke demanded, as he bit into his potato.

'The messenger, my lord?' Lascal moved

forward, thinking on his feet. Sometimes he had to work hard to keep up with his masters.

'From the war,' the second Duke whined.

'The great war,' the third explained. 'He ought to be here.'

Lascal coughed nervously. The Dukes had been expecting a messenger for some days now and he didn't dare disappoint them. 'He's . . . er . . . late, my lords,' he muttered.

'Well, we can see that,' the first lord sniffed. 'We're not stupid you know.'

Lascal waved at the servant with the water who stepped round (avoiding the shower of rain) and refilled the goblets.

'Yes, more wine,' the second lord said, sadly. It looked as if the messenger was never going to come.

But just then there was a pounding on the castle gate that echoed throughout the building. Lascal's head snapped round. He had not been expecting anybody that night. Could it have been the thunder? But then the knocking started again, and the first Duke looked up and smiled.

'That must be him now!' he exclaimed.

'Quite!' the second Duke agreed.

'It must be!' the third Duke added.

It took Lascal a few moments to recover. He had not planned it. So it could be dangerous. He was uncertain what to do.

'Well, see to it, Lascal,' the first Duke snapped.

Whoever it was would have to die. It was as

simple as that. He would kill the 'messenger' himself and tell the Dukes that the man had died of exhaustion on the doorstep or had arrived wounded (from the great war) and succumbed to his injuries. They would believe him. They always believed him. Bowing to the lords, he strode out of the great hall and down the corridor that led to the castle doors. A soldier had already opened them and a man was standing there, dripping wet, his horse behind him.

Lascal's hand reached for the dagger he wore in his belt. Unlike the wine and the meat, the dagger was real. 'Who are you?' he demanded. 'What do you want?'

'Shelter,' William Tell said, 'from the storm.'

'Shelter?'

'I just need a roof. Until daylight.'

Lascal tried to catch the attention of the soldier out of the corner of his eye. This didn't look like the sort of man who would die easily. It would need two of them. 'A beggar . . .' he sneered.

'I can pay,' Tell offered.

'You think this is some sort of tavern?'

'No. Taverns are usually more hospitable.'

'Then find one. You can't stay here.'

The soldier had understood. He was standing behind the stranger, slowly sliding his sword out of his sheath. Lascal smiled. This was going to be easy after all. They would bury the man in the morning and keep his horse. He might even find a use for the animal. The Dukes had been complaining for weeks that they wanted to hunt . . . forgetting that they had no horses of their own and anyway could barely stand, let alone ride.

The sword was raised. Lascal nodded. Cut him down from behind. Do it now. But then the soldier hesitated, his face falling and Lascal turned round. The three Dukes had staggered away from the table and followed him. They were standing in the corridor, beaming at the stranger. He was too late.

'The messenger,' the first Duke cried.

'At last!' the second exclaimed.

'So what's the message?' the third asked. 'Make him tell us, Lascal.'

William Tell had been about to move. He had known too much trouble not to be able to recognize it when he saw it and had been aware of the armed soldier from the moment he had entered the castle. Another second and his own knife would have been out. The soldier would have been cut down before he could move and then it would have been the steward's turn. But the situation had changed with the appearance of the three ancient men. They were the ones in control. He heard the soldier slide his weapon back into its sheath and his own hand fell back to his side.

'The war!' the first Duke insisted.

'What news of the war?' the second demanded.

'The war?' It was news to Tell. As far as he

knew, there hadn't been a war in the Empire for almost a hundred years.

'The great war,' the third Duke explained. 'What's the news?'

There was another embarrassed pause as Tell took this all in. Then Lascal tried to seize the advantage. 'This isn't the messenger, my lords,' he said.

'Isn't it?' the first Duke asked.

'Yes, I am.'

Tell had worked it out – and just in time. The three men were either senile or mad. Or both. They evidently believed that there was some sort of war going on and had been expecting news from the front. The man they called Lascal was probably as mad as they were . . . either that or he was feeding their madness for some reason of his own. He had been about to kill Tell. But so long as Tell pretended to be the expected messenger, he was safe. And all he wanted was a few hours' sanctuary. As soon as the storm had passed he would be on his way.

'I am the messenger,' he said.

'There you are!' The first lord stepped forward. 'I am Claud.'

'I'm Clarence.'

'And I'm Clovis.'

'So how's the war going?'

Tell shrugged. 'Well . . . it's going pretty well.'

There was a long silence. Evidently the Dukes had been expecting more but how could Tell give them news of a war that existed only in their own imagination? Fortunately, however, they decided to give him some breathing space.

'He's tired,' Clovis said.

'Exhausted,' Claud added.

'Exactly,' Clarence agreed. Propped up between the two other men, he wagged his head at the steward. 'Give him a room, Lascal. We'll talk to him in the morning.'

'In the morning.'

'Yes. In the morning.'

The three old men shuffled round in the draughty corridor and went back the way they had come. Tell was left face to face with Lascal. The steward was furious. This stranger wasn't only strong, he was also quick-witted. He had to go. But for the time being, there was nothing he could do. 'We'll have your horse stabled,' he scowled. 'You come with me.'

Without another word, Lascal led him through the castle. As Tell followed, he looked around him. From outside, in the storm, it had looked huge and impregnable. Now that he was inside, he could see that it was falling apart. Here and there, beams of wood supported the ceiling which was itself full of holes, letting in the rain. The floor was uneven, a patchwork of cracked marble, damp soil and straw. Weeds sprouted through the brickwork and the torches that lined the walls hadn't burnt in years. One hundred years ago, the castle might have been grand and impressive. Now it was just waiting for an excuse to fall down.

He was taken up a flight of steps, the whole staircase leaning away from the wall. Upstairs, the floor was pitted with gaps where the boards had rotted away. Lascal didn't give him any warning. The steward would have been delighted if his uninvited guest had plunged through one of the holes and broken his neck below. At last they reached a door, the most solid door Tell had seen so far.

'You can stay here,' Lascal said.

'Thank you.' Tell couldn't keep the sarcasm out of his voice.

Lascal opened the door. There was no furniture inside the room, only a blanket and a heap of straw. 'Don't try and leave the room,' he said. 'My soldiers know how to deal with intruders.' He nodded at the straw. 'I'd get some sleep if I were you.' He smiled grimly. 'You're going to have some explaining to do tomorrow morning.'

Tell went into the room. The door closed behind him. He waited a few moments, then tried it. As he had suspected, it was locked. He walked across the floor and looked out of the window. It gave out into a large enclosed courtyard. It was still raining. There were four soldiers out there, dragging something across the paving stones. The lightning flickered and Tell saw a blood-streaked hand, sliding lifelessly along the ground. Two bodies. Both wrapped in blankets.

He waited until the dead men had been carried out. Then he lay down and tried to get some sleep.

'But what of the eastern front?' Clovis demanded.

'The northern front?' Claud asked.

'The western front?' Clovis sighed.

The meeting was not going well. As soon as he had woken up, Tell had searched for an opportunity to get out of the castle. But Lascal had been waiting for him. From the moment he had left the room he had been escorted by a dozen soldiers. They were in the great hall now, all around him. Their crossbows looked old and battered. But Tell had no doubt that if he didn't pull something off soon, they would cut him down where he stood.

'You seem remarkably ill-informed . . .' Clovis muttered.

'. . . for a messenger,' Claud completed the sentence.

Next to the Dukes, Lascal rubbed his hands. A few more questions and this 'messenger' would be discredited once and for all. After that, there would have to be a judgement. He had already worked out the sentence.

'Well . . .' Tell coughed. 'The eastern front is looking pretty good.'

'A victory?' Clarence asked hopefully.

'A great victory!'

The three lords clapped their hands together excitedly. This was the best news they had heard in ten years. But then it was the only news they had heard in ten years. 'What about Marshal Ney?' one of them asked.

'Oh . . . Marshal Ney?' Tell smiled vaguely while he tried to work out an answer. 'He's a terrific soldier,' he muttered.

Claud's face fell. 'But he's the enemy!'

'Is he? Of course he is! Yes. But when I said just now that he's a terrific soldier, I meant that he's a terrific *dead* soldier. Which is to say, he's dead . . . and that's terrific!'

'Dead?' Clarence stared at Clovis.

'That's impossible!' Clovis stared at Claud.

'Well . . . it's rumoured that he's dead.' Tell gazed at the three Dukes who were now muttering amongst themselves. 'We were just as surprised as you,' he added.

The three Dukes straightened up in their seats.

'None of your answers make any sense,' Claud said.

'None at all,' Clarence agreed.

Lascal snapped to attention, waiting for the order that would be Tell's death warrant. But the Dukes had not yet made up their minds. This was a new situation for them too.

'Have him taken to his room, Lascal,' Clovis ordered. 'We must discuss this at length.'

Lascal cursed quietly as Tell was once again led out of the great hall. It had gone on long enough. Everything about the man spelled danger and the sooner he was put down the better. But Lascal had been thinking about it during the night. He had a plan.

'It's very strange,' Claud was saying. 'I don't think he's a messenger at all.'

'He *said* he was a messenger,' Clovis reminded him.

'But he isn't,' Claud insisted.

'Then who is he?' Clarence asked.

Lascal coughed. 'My lords, I think I may have an answer to that.'

The three heads creaked round on their three withered necks as Lascal approached them. He was holding a sheet of paper which he had prepared early that morning. Now he unfolded it. 'Last night, my lords,' he began, 'while he was asleep, I searched through his belongings. There was a secret compartment in his horse . . .'

'In his horse?'

'. . . in his saddlebag and I came across certain papers. It seems that this man has lied to us.'

'Then who is he?' Clovis asked.

'He is a spy, my lords, sent here as a messenger by Marshal Ney himself.' Lascal tapped the paper. 'These are his instructions. His purpose is to confuse us . . . to feed us false information about the war.'

None of the Dukes asked to see the paper. One of them had never been able to read and the other two, who had once been able to, had since forgotten how. Lascal knew this. He could have waved a shopping list at them and the result would have been the same.

'A spy,' Clovis muttered.

'I thought so,' Claud said.

'Then get him, Lascal,' Clarence ordered. 'Bring him to us. We must judge him.'

Lascal smiled. 'As you wish, my lords . . .'

But William Tell was no longer in his room.

The moment the door had been closed and locked behind him he had moved to the window. He knew that his performance as the messenger had failed to impress the Dukes and that left to themselves they would soon decide he was an impostor. He didn't intend waiting to find out what would happen next.

There was a narrow ledge outside the window, no more than four inches wide, running the full length of the wall about fifteen feet above the courtyard. Resting his weight on the window, he lowered himself onto it. There was just room for his toes and an inch of his foot. His heels jutted out into space. Hugging the wall, he began to shuffle towards the next window, hoping that it would lead into a chamber with an open and unguarded door.

The ledge was weak, eaten away by rain and wind. He had taken no more than two hesitant steps when a great chunk of it came away, crumbling down into the courtyard below. At the same moment, two soldiers walked out of an archway.

Tell froze. If they looked up, he was finished. But the two men were deep in conversation. Tell heard a few words as they walked past; something about a judgement and a bet. Then they were gone. With a sigh of relief, he moved again, his clothes rubbing against the coarse wall, his face pressed against the stone.

It took him a full ten minutes to cover the few feet to the next window but at last he reached it and pulled himself in. Now he found himself in a second chamber, identical to the one in which he had passed the night except that not only was the door unlocked but it wasn't even attached to the frame, leaning instead against the wall. He ducked his head out and looked back down the passage. There was no one in sight.

He stepped out. In the distance he heard voices – Lascal and soldiers. So he had only just moved in time. Sprinting back the other way, he turned a corner and climbed down a flight of stairs. There was a door at the bottom, bolted on his side. He opened it and passed through. The door led into an underground prison lined not with cells but with cages. There were a dozen cages in all, the barred doors fixed with heavy chains. Only one of the cages was occupied. A young man, well-dressed and good-looking stood, clutching the bars. Tell could see at a glance that he was, if not a nobleman, then the servant of a noble household. His clothes were expensive. His pale, thin face and delicate hands were more suited to an artist or musician than to a worker from the fields.

'Who are you?' the young man called out, seeing Tell. 'You're not one of them.'

'One of who?' Tell closed the door behind him and moved into the gloomy chamber.

'Help me get out of here?'

Tell turned his attention to the lock that fastened the cage. He might be able to spring it with his knife, but it would take time. 'How did you get here?' he asked. 'What have you done?'

'I haven't done anything,' the young man said. 'My name is Conrad. I was riding by, travelling through the valley. They captured me. I've been here . . . I don't know how long I've been here. They're going to kill me.'

Tell twisted the point of his knife in the lock. It refused to spring. 'What is going on in this place?' he demanded through gritted teeth.

'The three old men are the Dukes of Zahringen,' Conrad explained. 'Their family once ruled the whole Empire . . . but that was a hundred years ago. There was a war. They were defeated. Only a few survived.'

'The war,' Tell muttered, recalling Marshal Ney and his various fronts.

'They still think it's going on,' Conrad continued. 'Didn't you see them? They're insane . . . completely insane. And the steward – Lascal – he's as mad as they are. He's served them all his life, bringing people here to . . . feed their fantasies. Peasants, travellers . . . anyone. They're forced to fight duels. And then die.'

'What about you?' Tell asked. He turned the knife again and the lock clicked.

'I haven't fought yet. They've been saving me, I suppose.' Conrad pushed the door open. 'Thank you.' He took a deep breath. 'I thought I was never going to get out of here.'

'The spy and the traitor!'

Tell wheeled round. Lascal stood in the doorway, five armed soldiers behind him. There was no other way out of the prison.

'How good of you to open the cage,' he mocked. 'It will save me the trouble of finding the key.' He rubbed his hands together. 'You're both to come with me,' he said. 'It's time for the judgement.'

'Let the judgement begin.'

Once again the three Dukes were sitting in the courtyard. It had stopped raining, but the paving stones were still glistening wet. Lascal walked forward.

'There can be no denying the guilt of the accused,' he exclaimed. 'One is a spy who came like a snake among us to poison and to deceive. The other is a young soldier who chose to betray us for a handful of silver.' (Lascal was particularly proud of this piece of invention. It added a sense of drama to the fight that seemed particularly apt.) 'And yet,' he went on, 'we can still find it in our hearts to offer mercy. A trial by combat! One of them must die, but we will allow one of them to go free. Yes, Marshal Ney will see how the Dukes of Zahringen deal with their enemies . . .'

Tell and Conrad had heard all this from the pen where they were being kept on the side of the arena. As he had been led there, the strap tied to his wrist, Tell had noted the positions of the soldiers in the courtyard, which of them held crossbows and which merely carried swords. He had been left alone with Conrad for only a few minutes. Quickly, he whispered a plan.

'It'll never work,' Conrad said. 'We have to fight. We have no choice.'

'Listen to me, Conrad.' Tell stared at him with eyes that were suddenly ice. 'If you try to fight me, I'll kill you. If you believe nothing else, believe that.'

'And then they'll kill you,' Conrad said.

'Exactly. That's why we have to do it our way. They've given us knives. They expect us to use them on each other, but . . .'

He got no further. The soldiers had come for them. They were led out into the ring.

Lascal stood over them. 'A duel to the death, my lords,' he cried. 'The winner will be given his life.'

Tell and Conrad turned to confront one another.

They had each been given a butcher's knife, the same knives that the peasants had used only the day before. Like the peasants, they were joined at the wrist by a leather band. Tell had already examined it and knew that it would take him time to cut through it with the knife. And in that time the soldiers would kill him – always assuming that Conrad didn't. He glanced at the boy. Conrad's lips were drawn and his eyes narrow. He was circling round Tell, his knife held low. To all appearances, he was manoeuvring for position, on the point of launching an attack. Only Tell knew differently. He had listened to what Tell had said. He was playing it Tell's way.

Tell slashed forward, the blow carefully aimed to look convincing but do no harm. The blade passed a few inches over Conrad's head. At the same time, Conrad stabbed forward. Tell twisted to one side. The knife didn't even come close.

Both men paused as if catching their breath. Carefully, Tell looked around him. There were two men with crossbows only a few feet away. They were the real danger. One false move and they would fire – and at that range it would be difficult to miss. Two more soldiers had crossbows, but they had been badly positioned, high up on the battlements . . . a difficult shot even if the target wasn't moving. The three Dukes were in the distance, seated on their absurd thrones. Tell ignored them. That just left Lascal, standing on a raised step just beneath the window of Tell's room. Lascal was the key. He was in control. If he gave the orders, the soldiers would obey.

Tell swept his knife through the air again. Conrad dodged, then pulled him round, swinging him on the end of the leather strap. It was exactly as they had planned. Tell had been brought closer to Lascal. He was facing one of the crossbow-carrying soldiers. Conrad was only inches away from the other. This had to be the moment.

'Now!' Tell shouted.

They acted as one. Tell flipped his knife over and threw it. It looped once in the air, then found its target in the nearest soldier. Conrad turned and, using the handle of the knife, knocked the second soldier out. Then they ran forward towards Lascal. One of the soldiers on the battlements fired at them and missed. They reached Lascal. Tell whipped the leather cord around Lascal's neck. Conrad did the same. Before he knew what had happened, Lascal was standing between them, the leather cord around his neck.

Tell tightened his grip. 'Call off the guards, Lascal,' he shouted. 'Call them off or I break your neck.'

Lascal waved frantically with his arms. He couldn't talk. He could scarcely breathe.

Tell looked around him. Nobody moved. Only the three Dukes, shaking with fear and incomprehension, had tottered to their feet and were making their way back into the castle. 'We're walking out of here,' Tell said to Lascal. 'Together.'

There was nothing anybody could do. With

Lascal pinned between them, Conrad and Tell left the courtyard and followed the passage back to the main gates of the castle. While Tell kept a firm hold on Lascal, Conrad unbarred the gate and then they were out, following the castle wall around to a stable leaning against the brickwork. There was a forge here with a furnace still burning. Tell's horse had been tethered beside Conrad's.

An axe lay on the floor. Tell picked it up and cut through the leather strap with one blow. Lascal sank to his knees, gasping for breath.

'Come on,' Tell said. 'Let's ride out of here.'

But Lascal wasn't finished yet. As Tell turned his back on him and checked his saddle, his hand reached out for the axe. Then he was on his feet again, running towards him.

'Look out!' Conrad shouted.

Tell spun round. There was a knife in his hand. He had heard Lascal and had pulled it out of its sheath below the saddle as he turned. He didn't even need to aim. Lascal, running forward and carried by his own momentum, impaled himself on the blade. With a thin whine, Lascal dropped the axe and crumpled.

Tell looked at the body with a grimace of distaste. There was a log jutting out of the furnace and, snatching it up, he hurled it high in the air, over the castle wall.

'Places like that shouldn't be allowed to stand,' he said.

He got onto his horse and, without waiting for Conrad, rode out into the open air.

The flames were sweeping through the castle now. The stonework might be fireproof but the wooden props, the straw and the mouldy tapestries sprang alight as if they had been looking forward to the moment.

The three Dukes were back in the banqueting hall, being served another meal of potatoes and water. The minstrels were playing. The jugglers were attempting to juggle. Nobody seemed to notice the smoke that was filling the air. Nobody seemed to hear the crackle of the approaching flames.

'Maybe he was a messenger,' Clovis said, jabbing a fork into his potato.

'I don't think he was a messenger,' Claud muttered.

'He said we were winning,' Clarence reminded them.

A shower of rubble tumbled down from the ceiling and for a moment the minstrels disappeared altogether. When the dust settled again, one of them was lying on his back. Another was attempting to pluck at a harp that no longer had any strings. Clovis lifted his goblet and sniffed his water. 'A good wine,' he murmured. 'But not a great wine.'

'Not like the war,' Claud said, sipping his own water.

'No,' Clovis agreed. 'It's a great war.'

Clovis reached for the jug and offered it to Clarence. 'More wine?' he asked.

The fire had burnt away the wooden props. A great slab of stone plummeted down from the ceiling. It landed on Clarence. Claud looked at the body sadly. 'I don't think he wants any more wine,' he said.

The two remaining Dukes drank and feasted while their castle collapsed around them.

Eight: The Champion

William Tell rode with Conrad for the next few days, their journey taking them ever further south. It turned out that Conrad had been on his way to the town of Ursen when he was seized by the Dukes of Zahringen . . . and Ursen was of particular interest to Tell. Once again he thought back to the banquet at Gessler's castle, the moment when he had been ordered to shoot the apple off his son's head. There had been an elderly man, sitting with his wife at the end of the table. The man had said nothing but his face had spoken volumes. And Tell had recognized him. Once, a few years before, he had mended a sword for the man. He was the Governor of Ursen.

If he could meet with this Governor, Tell might be able to get the one thing he wanted most: news of his son. The last time he had seen Matthew, the boy had been tied to the pole, in a dead faint. Gessler had refused to tell him what had happened next. He had tricked his wife into believing that the boy was dead. But Tell was certain he was alive. He could feel it as surely as he could feel his own heart. Matthew was alive. He would find him.

He remembered what he had heard about the Governor of Ursen. He was said to be a world apart from Gessler. Although they shared the same rank, Ursen governed his province with fairness and even generosity. The taxes were high. They had to be when the Emperor set the level. But Ursen took his revenues from the rich and poor alike – and he hadn't built himself magnificent castles or palaces along the way. Ursen's loathing of Gessler had been clear for all to see at the banquet. Could Tell use that loathing to suit his own ends?

'. . . and the first prize is a hundred gold marks.'

Tell realized that Conrad had been talking for the past ten minutes and he hadn't heard a word of it. In the few days they had been riding together, he had come to like the young nobleman. For that was what Conrad was . . . at least in name. A title was all he had left. His wealth and lands had been stripped from him, another victim of Gessler's greed.

He was on his way to Ursen to take part in a shooting competition. Apparently it was an annual event, each province taking part in a sort of league table until only two finalists were left. From these a champion would emerge to receive a purse of one hundred gold marks, and most likely, a position in the castle of the Governor whose team he represented.

Gessler had won for the past five years

running. His champion was a man known only as North, named after the country he had supposedly come from, somewhere in the north. One other thing was known about North. He never missed.

'The teams are named after birds,' Conrad explained. 'Ursen's team is the hawks. Gessler's is the ravens. There are usually about six teams taking part but I expect most of them will have been knocked out by now.' He sighed. 'I was hoping to shoot with the hawks. If I'd won the purse it would have meant a new start for me.'

'You're a good shot?' Tell asked.

Conrad shook his head sadly. 'No. That's the trouble. I'm all right at close range, but they use moving targets and they get further away at every stage of the competition.' They rode on for a few minutes in silence. 'How about you?' Conrad asked. 'Can you shoot a crossbow?'

Tell shrugged. 'Yes.'

'Then why don't you enter the competition? I'd love to see the smile knocked off Gessler's face if you won.'

Tell would have liked to have seen Gessler too, but not just to beat him at a game. He was not a man who enjoyed killing, but he would enjoy killing Gessler, settling the score for once and for all. It had to be done. If Tell didn't kill Gessler, then one day Gessler would kill Tell. He had been forced into a game of a very different sort and it was Gessler who had made up the rules. Only the death of one of them would bring that game to an end.

'I can't enter the competition,' he said.

'Why not?' Conrad waited for an answer but Tell didn't speak. 'Look,' he went on. 'You saved my life, but I don't know anything about you. You haven't even told me your name. Maybe it's none of my business, but whenever I mention Gessler I see something strange in your eyes. Something frightening. So why don't you *use* the tournament? He'll be there. You can use it to finish whatever there is between you . . . and bring him down a peg or two at the same time.'

'I can't be seen in Ursen,' Tell said.

'You don't have to be. I've told you. The teams are named after birds. And all the contestants wear masks. Nobody has ever seen North's face. Nobody need see yours either.'

'Masks?' Tell thought for a moment in silence. A shooting contest. A huge prize. Gessler. A champion. Why not?

Smiling, he spurred his horse on.

The city of Ursen had been built inside a massive stone wall with towers at every corner, fortified against possible attack. Only one gate led in, surmounted by a portcullis that could be lowered at the first cry from the look-out posts. From the outside, it was a grim place – the grey stone punctuated only by the narrow slits through which concealed archers could fire. It stood on a slope, commanding the entire valley with the mountains rising up behind it like a second wall of defence.

Inside, however, it was quite different. The various buildings had been packed tightly together – necessarily, because of the limited space – and this had created a maze of narrow streets surmounted by shadowy arches. For the festival, these streets had been decked with flags and flowers. Banners, with the head of a hawk, hung from every window and hawk-dolls, hawk badges and even gingerbread hawks were being sold in every street-side stall. There was only one open space in the city, a great square right at the heart. This was where the governor's home stood. On most days of the week, the entire ground would be covered with an open-air market. There were still dozens of stalls all round the edge of the square but now the central area had been cleared to make way for the targets. This year, the hawks had made it through to the final. Not surprisingly, they would be competing against Gessler's ravens.

It was the evening before the last day of the tournament, and by tradition, the Governor of Ursen had opened his doors to the opposing team. It hurt him to see Gessler sitting in his banqueting hall, drinking his wine and devouring his food. Gessler's champion was sitting beside him, barely eating anything. And his new commander, Horse or Horst or something like that, was standing behind him, gazing at the company with a blank face and ugly, black eyes.

'Your health, Ursen!' Gessler raised his goblet, spilling red wine over his hand. 'I must say, you've had a lot of luck, reaching the final.'

'Luck?'

'And skill, of course. Not that it'll help you tomorrow. Five years I've been coming here and North has never lost.' Gessler yawned. 'It's almost too predictable.'

The Governor of Ursen was sitting next to his wife, Elizabeth, and once again she stretched out a hand to restrain him. Gessler had been needling him all evening. Every word he spoke, the very way he sat, swaggering in his chair, seemed designed to offend. There was something nasty in the air, she could tell. She had heard that Gessler was badly in debt, that he had failed to raise the taxes necessary to pay the Emperor. He was planning something, and this banquet was part of it. She just hoped that her husband would have the strength to ignore him.

'What makes you so sure your champion will win tomorrow?' Ursen demanded, his eyes flashing with anger.

'You don't really think you have a chance, do you?' Gessler mocked.

'Of course.'

'And would you be prepared to bet on it?'

There was a sudden hush in the room. About two hundred people were seated along the four long tables and all of them were looking at Ursen. The Governor had gone very pale . . . with anger, not fear.

'Of course I'll bet with you, Gessler,' he said.

'My dear . . .' Elizabeth began.

'Your wife seems to be afraid for you,' Gessler muttered.

'What bet do you have in mind, Gessler?'

'A full year of tax revenues. Yours against mine.'

An astonished buzz went round the room. What Gessler was proposing was monstrous, insane. Losing the competition would almost certainly mean losing the Governorship. No man could part with such a huge sum and hope to continue in office.

'It's supposed to be a friendly competition,' Ursen said. 'It's not about money. It's about sportsmanship.'

'Of course,' Gessler shrugged, 'if you're afraid . . .'

'I'm not afraid.'

'Then bet!'

'Done!'

Ursen had uttered the word before he knew what he was saying. And now, out of the corner of his eye, he saw Horst smile for the first time and realized what a fool he had been. Gessler had been working on him from the moment he had arrived, had been building it up all along. He turned round and looked at his wife. Elizabeth was staring at him as if he had just died. And that's just what I have done, he thought to himself. Gessler laughed and reached out for more wine. The Governor of Ursen slumped back in his chair. There could be no backing out now. Two hundred people had been witness to the bet. He just had to hope that his champion would shoot straight.

Ursen got no sleep that night and the following morning found him walking back and forth across the tournament area, wondering how he could have been so gullible. Perhaps he had drunk too much. Certainly he had talked too much. He had a good team. He knew it. Even reaching second place was an achievement in itself. But he had no single marksman who could take on North and in the final contest, one against one, he knew he would be beaten.

There were few people about in the chill morning light. One or two servants were preparing the ground, carrying out targets and sweeping away the litter. They avoided the Governor. The whole town had heard the news by now and despite the gay banners and decorations, the mood was one of gloom. He was doomed – and that meant they were doomed with him. A new Governor would bring new laws. The peaceful life of Ursen was about to be shattered for ever.

The Governor knew this too and it hurt him more than anything. He had failed his people.

One moment of stupidity had destroyed the work of a lifetime.

'My lord . . . ?'

He looked up. Two men were standing in front of him. One was short and dark, a nobleman from the looks of him and unknown to the Governor. The other was standing behind him, keeping his head bowed as if afraid of being recognized. But the Governor did recognize him and with that recognition came the first stirrings of hope.

'We want to take part in the contest,' the younger man said.

'Who are you?' the Governor asked.

'My name is Conrad. This is . . .' Conrad hesitated. He still didn't know Tell's name.

'Names don't matter here,' the Governor cut in. 'All that matters is marksmanship. Can you shoot?'

'I can shoot,' Tell said.

The Governor glanced upwards. High above him, jutting out of a church tower, there was a gargoyle, made of wood, its mouth open. He pointed at it. 'Show me,' he said. 'The gargoyle. That's your target.'

Tell was carrying his crossbow. Now he loaded it and lifted it to aim at the gargoyle. It was a difficult shot. The target was small and the slanting light made it almost invisible. Worse still, the upward angle reduced any chance of accuracy. But if this man was who the Governor thought he was, he would hit the target without even hesitating.

A second later the bolt slammed straight into the gaping mouth. Conrad had fired at the same time. He was a good shot, but his aim had been a few inches off. His bolt broke against the brickwork and clattered to the ground.

The Governor smiled, feeling the relief wash over him. 'Get yourself masks,' he said. 'You'll be shooting with the hawks.'

Tell and Conrad bowed and moved away, but the Governor called out to them again. 'You,' he said, addressing Tell. 'Wait a moment.'

Conrad shrugged and continued towards the competitor's tent at the edge of the square. Tell remained where he was.

'You're William Tell,' the Governor said, simply.

Tell said nothing.

'You want to kill Gessler.'

Still Tell didn't speak but the Governor could see the answer in his eyes.

'What happened to you was a terrible injustice,' he said. 'I'm ashamed of it. But I cannot allow you to take revenge on my land. Right now, as far as I'm concerned, you've committed no crime. All that will change if you decide to take action. I understand your quarrel with Gessler. God knows I understand it. But I still want your word that you will not pursue it. Not while you're here.'

Tell nodded almost imperceptibly. 'You have

it, Governor,' he said. 'But there's something I want in return.'

'Name it.'

'Tell me what happened to Matthew. Where can I find my son?'

The Governor closed his eyes and for a moment he was back in Gessler's castle, at the banquet to honour Prince Frederick's visit. He remembered the father and son being brought in, Gessler's gloating cruelty. He knew now that Gessler used people for his own pleasure, destroying them without a second thought. But then he had been horrified. He had been unable to watch the challenge, at the same time unable to tear his eyes away from it. Tell had fired, had hit the apple. The boy had fainted. Tell had been knocked down by Tyrrol. And then . . .

He opened his eyes.

'Prince Frederick's son – Martin – took pity on him. When the royal entourage left, they took your son with them. To the Citadel.'

'The Citadel?'

'At Aargau. The home of the Emperor.'

'He's a prisoner there? In the dungeons?'

'A prisoner, yes.' The Governor nodded. 'But from what I've heard, he's living in the palace, a sort of companion to the prince.'

Tell raised a hand to his eyes. It was as if a great weight had been lifted from his shoulders. At last he had heard real news about Matthew. At last he had something to live for.

'Don't worry about Gessler,' he said. 'I've heard about your bet and I'm not planning to kill him.' He smiled mirthlessly. 'He's got too much to lose.'

The contest began later that day.

A stand had been erected along one side of the square and it was here that Gessler, Ursen and the visiting dignitaries sat. Opposite them, the townspeople and peasants jostled for position, shouting encouragement at their favourites while hawkers and pedlars ran up and down, selling their wares. The third side of the square had been given over to the targets and the teams were ranged along the fourth, standing in front of their tents which shone a dazzling white in the bright sunlight.

Gessler was in a good mood, a mood that became all the better as the ravens moved swiftly into the lead. He was sitting back with a goblet of wine in his hand, his head crowned by an absurd hat, thick blue velvet complete with feather. He had almost forgotten the two hundred silver pieces he had paid De Flores and the numerous other problems in his own province. He had no doubt that North would win. After all, North had never lost. And he would leave Ursen with a year's taxes taken care of and the pleasure of having humiliated his arrogant and priggish host.

There were two teams with six archers in each.

All of them were masked, but it was easy to see when North was shooting. Every bolt he fired found the bull's eye, adding to the ravens' score. In this part of the contest, three targets were used. The first was a standard disc with three red circles. The second was attached to a rope and swung like a pendulum. The third rolled down a wooden rail, only visible to the marksmen for a few seconds. None of these targets was any problem to North.

'Confident, Governor?' Gessler asked, leaning towards Ursen.

'I may surprise you yet, Gessler,' Ursen replied.

For the first time. Gessler was uneasy. The Governor of Ursen was relaxed, chatting with his wife, occasionally pointing towards the archers. Something was wrong. The man couldn't win. He had to know that. So why wasn't he more afraid?

Gessler glanced at the scoreboard, a brightly coloured panel of wood with the two symbols, ravens and hawks, painted above the scores. A few moments before it had read: RAVENS 26 HAWKS 19. Now an attendant was changing the numbers. When he looked again, it read: RAVENS 29 HAWKS 25.

He looked again at the archers and his eyes narrowed. He had stopped breathing without even knowing quite why. One of the six men in hawk masks had just fired, the bolt driving into the very centre of the target. Gessler couldn't see his face, but there was something about the way the man stood, the way he held his crossbow that reminded him . . .

Where had he seen that man before?

He watched as the figure fired two more bolts. All three found their target and yet they had been fired almost effortlessly. The crowd was applauding him. They had seen it too. This man was different. He had not been in the arena the day before. He had come from nowhere and he was dangerous. Gessler turned back to the scoreboard and stared. A bead of sweat trickled down the side of his face. RAVENS 32 HAWKS 31.

William Tell.

It had to be.

Nobody else could shoot like that.

The Governor of Ursen was smiling. 'What is it, Gessler? You've gone quite pale. Was it something you ate?'

'Who is he?' Gessler demanded. 'The tall one. Third from the left.'

Ursen pretended to scrutinize the archers. 'I can't remember his name,' he said. 'But he's quite a good shot.'

By the end of the morning session, the hawks and the ravens were level, both with thirty-five. There would be a break for refreshments and then the contest would be decided with a play-off: Gessler's champion against Ursen's. The excitement in the crowd was almost out of control.

It was being whispered that the Governor had found himself a magician, that the mysterious archer was enchanted. People were saying that the Governor of Ursen had been keeping him in reserve all along and that he had only made his bet with Gessler knowing that he would win. Already casks of mead were being broached and the celebrations prepared. A full year of tax revenues! What Ursen stood to win made even the one-hundred-gold-piece purse shrink into insignificance.

Gessler was furious. While the other Governors sipped their wine and chewed on legs of roast chicken, he sought out Horst, his face dark with menace. 'It's William Tell,' he insisted. 'Find him, Horst. Get a look at his face. Then come back and tell me.'

Meanwhile, Tell was sitting in the hawks' tent, his mask beside him. Conrad was with him, and for once the young man was gloomy.

'You never told me you could shoot like that,' he said.

'You never asked me.' Tell's mind was concentrated on the ordeal ahead. He had been watching North shoot. He knew they were evenly matched.

'Ah well . . . I suppose I should never even have dreamt I could be the champion. But I can tell you now, I wouldn't have minded getting my hands on that purse.'

'It may not be too late.'

'What do you mean?' Conrad threw his own mask onto the ground. 'You've been chosen as Ursen's champion. You're the one who's going to win!'

There was a movement outside the tent. At once Tell was on his feet, moving towards the opening. As he had suspected, Horst was slipping away. He had been listening to the entire conversation. Perhaps he had even glimpsed Tell through the open tent-flap. Tell watched him go, the beginnings of a smile on his face.

'Who was that?' Conrad asked.

'An old friend,' Tell replied.

'Did he see you?'

'I expect so.'

'And you're not worried?'

Tell walked back into the tent and sat down. 'I was expecting him. Now listen, Conrad. Listen very carefully . . .'

When Gessler took his place for the last leg of the tournament, he was confident once again. Horst had indeed seen Tell. And knowing that, Gessler knew that he couldn't lose.

For even if Tell won the competition, Ursen would lose the prize. Tell was an outlaw, a criminal. The moment he had fired his last bolt, Gessler would have him arrested – and Ursen along with him, for harbouring a wanted man. Gessler would take the prize money. He would take the year's taxes. If everything went his way, he might even take the whole province. For the first time that day Gessler felt entirely at ease. Whatever happened, the tournament would finish with a hanging. And William Tell would trouble him no more.

The crowd applauded as the two masked contestants, the hawk and the raven, stepped out of their tents and walked ten yards forward to take their places opposite the final target. This was a tiny disc with two rings hanging in front of it. The rings would be swung in towards each other, overlapping for perhaps one second. It was at that moment that the archers were to fire, their bolt passing between the two rings, locking them together, pinning them to the centre of the target. For this, the last contest, the range was greater than ever. The archers had been kept well back, away from the spectators. The sun was behind them. Gessler squinted as they loaded their bows and prepared to fire.

'You look more confident, Gessler,' Ursen said.

'I am confident, Governor,' Gessler replied.

'You may be surprised.'

'Not as surprised as you're going to be, Governor.'

The rings were swung, back and forth over the target.

Both men fired at the same moment. A white bolt and a black bolt.

A referee ran forward. The crowd waited.

Then he turned round, raising the white arrow.

The hawk's shot had passed directly through the two rings and into the centre of the target. The raven's bolt had been half an inch to the left.

The hawks had won.

The crowd cheered and applauded. The Governor of Ursen stood up to have his hand shaken by all the friends who surrounded him. He looked back for Gessler, but already the other man was moving, striding across the square to where the single figure of the hawk stood waiting. Horst had gone with him and before anyone could stop him he had grabbed hold of the new champion.

The crowd fell silent once again. The Governor of Ursen hurried forward with his wife. Even in the moment of victory, he had been afraid of this. Somehow his opponent had guessed. He was about to unmask William Tell.

'This man is an outlaw!' Gessler shouted out. 'And the Governor of Ursen is a traitor for harbouring him. The contest is void. I win the bet and the hundred gold marks are mine.'

Gessler reached out for the hawk mask.

'William Tell!' he announced.

The mask came away.

But it was not William Tell who stood there, even though the man was wearing William Tell's clothes and had shot with William Tell's skill.

'That's no way to treat the champion of the tournament,' he said. 'And my name's not William Tell. It's Conrad.'

The Governor of Ursen stared at him, as surprised as Gessler. It was impossible. Only William Tell could have shot like that. Conrad hadn't even been able to hit the gargoyle on the church. But the Governor had seen him do it with his own eyes. It was impossible. Unless . . .

A second bolt was fired from nowhere. It caught the hat that Gessler was wearing and swept it off his head. Then the Governor understood.

Tell and Conrad had swapped clothes. While Conrad, wearing the mask, had stepped forward and taken his place opposite the targets, Tell had remained in the tent. It was incredible. He hadn't just beaten North. He had beaten him against impossible odds. For Conrad had only pretended to load his crossbow. Tell had fired the real shot *from inside the tent*, ten yards behind the other marksman. And that was where he was now.

Gessler had arrived at the same conclusion. With the laughter of the crowd ringing in his ears, he strode forward and threw open the tent. But it was empty. A slit ran down the canvas at the back. Tell had gone.

'My new champion!' he heard the Governor of Ursen say.

Conrad was standing next to him, holding up a sack of gold pieces. And how many more gold pieces would Gessler have to pay to settle his debt? Where would he find it? He was finished . . .

There were tears in his eyes as he plunged into the tent and out through the back. There was nobody in the street but in the distance, above the clamour of the crowd, he heard a horse's hooves, striking against the paving stones. Cursing and screaming, he ran on. The horse picked up speed. Gessler sank to his knees.

He had created William Tell. He had made him a legend. And in that single moment he had unwittingly destroyed himself.

Epilogue

Somewhere inside the Citadel, a bell chimed.

Matthew Tell walked slowly forward, shivering in the morning air. He no longer knew how long he had spent within the castle walls. The hours had turned to days and the days to weeks until eventually he had lost all track of time. He was a prisoner. He wore no chains and he slept in a bedroom rather than a cell – but there still could be no disguising the fact. If he refused an order, if he so much as raised his voice, he would be punished. If he now turned and made a run for the main gate, the guards would shoot him down before he had taken ten steps.

The Citadel was a fortress in the province of Aargau, the seat of the Emperor. All his power was concentrated here. It was the largest fortification in the country, a great pile of towers and battlements, of soaring stone walls and heavy iron gates. Fearful of his life, the Emperor had surrounded himself not by one squadron of soldiers or two but by an entire garrison. Nobody was allowed in without a special permit. Nobody could leave without the express royal command.

There was one exception to the rule: the pilgrims. A holy spring bubbled up in a well in one of the Citadel's courtyards; it was said that its waters had the powers to cure diseases. And once a year, for one week only, the courtyard was opened to the sick and the crippled, to anyone with the strength or enough friends to help them make the journey. The Emperor liked to think of the spring as a symbol of his own benevolence. What he didn't mention was the fact that he charged each pilgrim ten gold pieces to visit the waters.

That was where Matthew was heading now, following the royal procession. Prince Martin, grandson of the Emperor and his only friend in the castle, walked a few paces ahead of him. Matthew's feelings towards him were mixed. On the one hand, the prince had saved him from almost certain death after Gessler's cruel game. But at what cost? Matthew had become his servant, his page. Even now Matthew could not accept the injustice. The two boys were the same age. If anything, Matthew was the faster and the stronger of the two. So why should it be that an accident of birth should make one a master and the other a servant? Once, he had talked about fighting, about standing up for his rights. He – virtually alone – had refused to bow to the hat. But now his life had become no more than a constant humiliation.

His mind went back to Clairmont, his home

and his family. And not for the first time he had to force back the wave of despair that rose up within him, as solid and as crushing as the grey walls that surrounded him. He would never get out of the Citadel. He would still be there as an old man, sweeping the floors, being laughed at by the palace children. Now, when it was too late, he understood what his father had been trying to tell him. In Clairmont he had had a sort of freedom. There had been injustices. The world had been far from perfect. But if he had only looked, he would have found that freedom within himself. In Clairmont at least he had been his own man.

He heard chanting ahead of him and looked up. They had reached the well. A group of monks stood beside it, handing out phials of the precious water to the waiting pilgrims. The Emperor was moving amongst them, a condescending hand raised in greeting. As Matthew watched, a man brushed past him, leaning heavily on a crutch, his face hooded, a dirty patch covering one eye.

Matthew stepped aside, assuming that the man would limp forward to take his place in the queue. But the man stayed where he was. He wasn't even looking at the well. He was looking at Matthew.

And then Matthew saw.

It was his father.

He had survived Gessler and Death Castle. Somehow he had crossed the land and reached the Citadel. Disguised as a pilgrim, he had managed to get through the main gate.

His father had come for him.

There could be no action now – not yet. There were too many soldiers around and all the pilgrims would have been searched for weapons on the way in. But he realized, with a surge of hope and excitement, that his father would have planned something and that whatever happened, his time in the Citadel was drawing to a close. And at the same time, he knew that he had not only been wrong about himself but about his father too. Back in the village he had seen only a common blacksmith, a man who seemed content to serve life rather than to make life serve him. He had heard the legend, but he hadn't believed it.

The chanting of the monks rose up and embraced him. The sun was shining above the castle walls. For the first time in his life, he was seeing William Tell.